Cotton Mather

Leaders of the Colonial Era

Lord Baltimore

Benjamin Banneker

William Bradford

Benjamin Franklin

Anne Hutchinson

Cotton Mather

William Penn

John Smith

Miles Standish

Peter Stuyvesant

Leaders of the Colonial Era

Cotton Mather

Dennis Abrams

CHELSEA HOUSE
PUBLISHERS
An imprint of Infobase Publishing

Chelsea House
An imprint of Infobase Publishing
132 West 31st Street
New York, NY 10001

Library of Congress Cataloging-in-Publication Data
Abrams, Dennis, 1960-
  Cotton Mather / Dennis Abrams.
      p. cm. — (Leaders of the colonial era)
  Includes bibliographical references and index.
  ISBN 978-1-60413-736-1 (hardcover)
  1. Mather, Cotton, 1663–1728—Juvenile literature. 2. Puritans—Massachusetts—
Biography—Juvenile literature. 3. Massachusetts—History—Colonial period,
ca. 1600–1775—Juvenile literature. I. Title. II. Series.
  F67.M43A25 2010
  973.2092—dc22
  [B]
                                        2010010715

You can find Chelsea House on the World Wide Web at
http://www.chelseahouse.com

Text design by Kerry Casey
Cover design by Keith Trego
Composition by EJB Publishing Services
Cover printed by Bang Printing, Brainerd, Minn.
Book printed and bound by Bang Printing, Brainerd, Minn.
Date printed: December 2010
Printed in the United States of America

10 9 8 7 6 5 4 3 2 1

This book is printed on acid-free paper.

All links and Web addresses were checked and verified to be correct at the time of publication. Because of the dynamic nature of the Web, some addresses and links may have changed since publication and may no longer be valid.

Contents

1

The Goodwin Family

Go tell Mankind, that there are Devils and Witches; and that tho those night-birds least appear where the Daylight of the Gospel comes, yet New England has had Examples of their Existence and Operation.

—Cotton Mather, *Memorable Providences, Relating to Witchcrafts and Possessions*

It was summer in the year 1688. Cotton Mather, the noted clergyman of Boston's famous North Church, was asked by a Boston mason named John Goodwin to visit his sick daughter. What Mather saw during the course of his first and then subsequent visits to the Goodwin family both astonished and amazed him. The children of Goodwin, deeply religious and well brought up, seemed to be under a kind of "spell."

Initially it was just one daughter who was affected with fits. When Mather tried to pray with the girl to ask that she be cured, the girl would go deaf and remain that way until the prayers had ended. Soon, three more of Goodwin's children became affected as well, suffering what appeared to be unspeakable physical and mental torture. What could be causing it? The "symptoms" were described by Mather in his first important book-length publication, *Memorable Providences, Relating to Witchcrafts and Possessions*, written in 1689.

> The variety of their tortures increased continually; and tho about Nine or Ten at Night they always had a Release from their miseries; and ate and slept all night . . . Sometimes they would be Deaf, sometimes Dumb, and sometimes Blind, and often, all this at once. One while their Tongues would be drawn down their Throats; another-while they would be pull'd out upon their Chins, to a prodigious length.
>
> They would have their Mouths opened unto such a Wideness, that their Jaws went out of joint; and anon they would **clap together** again with a Force like that of a strong Spring-Lock. The same would happen to their Shoulder-Blades, and their Elbows, and Hand-wrists, and several of their joints . . .
>
> They would make most piteous **out-cries**, that they were cut with Knives, and struck with Blows that they could not bear. Their Necks would be broken, so that their Neck-bone would seem dissolved unto them that felt after it; and yet on the sudden, it would become, again so stiff that there was no stirring of their Heads; yea, their Heads would be **twisted almost around**; and if main Force at any time obstructed a dangerous motion which they seem'd to be upon, they would roar exceedingly.

What was it that could cause such physical and mental anguish to the Goodwin children? To Cotton Mather and to others in his community, the answer was both simple and obvious. The children were under the spell of a witch. To the Puritans of seventeenth-century New England, it was an easy diagnosis to make. For them, witchcraft, the devil, and evil spirits were as real and as threatening as viruses and mental illnesses are to us today.

It was learned that the Goodwin family's troubles began when their oldest daughter questioned a laundry woman who was suspected of stealing the family's sheets. The washerwoman's mother, on hearing of the accusations, cursed the girl, who immediately began suffering from fits, followed shortly thereafter by her siblings.

The washerwoman's mother, Goody Glover, described by Mather in *Memorable Providences* as "an ignorant and a scandalous old Woman," was put on trial for bewitching the Goodwin children. Among the evidence presented were small dolls or puppets stuffed with goat hair that were found in the possession of the defendant. During questioning, Glover stated that when she wanted to cause harm to the objects of her anger, she would lick her finger and then touch the figures with her wet finger. When she demonstrated this in court, one of the Goodwin children watching the trial promptly fell into fits, or seizures.

Others testified against her as well. One neighbor swore in court that another neighbor had told her that she, too, had been bewitched by Goody Glover and had seen her coming down her chimney. After being examined by five court-appointed physicians who found her to be "sane," Glover was sentenced to death for being a witch.

It was thought that by doing so, the children would be released from their suffering. But before her execution by hanging, Glover warned that "the Children should not be relieved by her Death, for others had a hand in it as well as she." Her warning proved to be prophetic, as Mather later described in *Memorable Providences*:

The Fits of the Children yet more arriv'd unto such Motions as were beyond the Efficacy of any natural Distemper in the

World. They would **bark** at one another like Dogs, and again **purr** like so many Cats. They would sometimes complain, that they were in a red-hot Oven, sweating and panting at the same time unreasonably; Anon they would say, Cold water was thrown upon them, at which they would shiver very much. They would cry out of dismal Blowes with great Cudgels laid upon them; and tho' we saw no cudgels nor blowes, yet we could see the Marks left by them in Red Streaks upon their bodies afterward. And one of them would be roasted on an invisible Spit, run into his Mouth, and out at his Foot, he lying, and rolling, and groaning as if it had been so in the most sensible manner in the world; and then he would shriek, that Knives were cutting of him.

Mather went on to note that the children would even act as if they could fly, fluttering their arms like wings, "carried with an incredible Swiftness thro the Air, having but just their Toes now and then upon the ground, and their Arms waved like the Wings of a Bird."

In an effort to help (and to allow others to witness the events), Mather invited the oldest Goodwin child, thirteen-year-old Martha, to stay at his home along with his wife and children. At first, she behaved normally. But on the morning of November 20, as Mather noted in *Memorable Providences*, Martha cried out, "Ah, They have found me out! I thought it would be so!" and immediately fell into fits once again.

She would find herself choking on a ball as big as a small egg. When she attempted to eat a roasted apple, Mather noted, "her Teeth would be set, and sometimes, if she went to take it up her Arm would be made so stiff, that she would not possibly bring her hand to her Mouth: at last she said, 'Now They say, I shall eat it, if I eat it quickly,' and she nimbly ate it up."

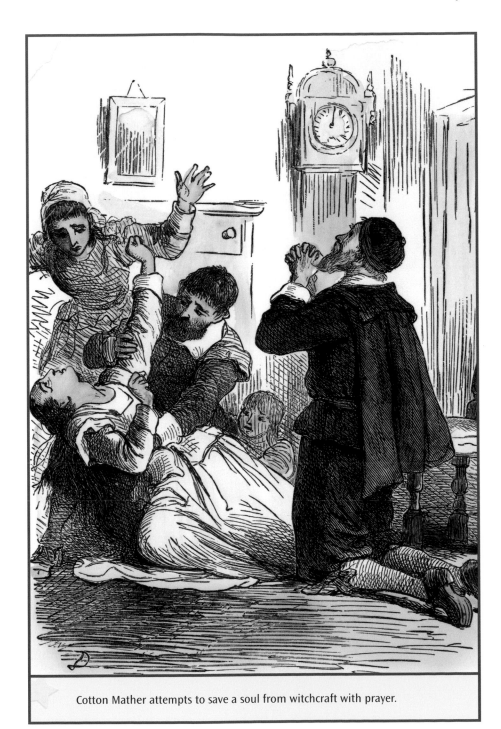

Cotton Mather attempts to save a soul from witchcraft with prayer.

MEDICAL CAUSES OF BEWITCHMENT

Today, there is general agreement that the girls claiming to be bewitched in the Goodwin family, as well as those in the Salem witch trials, were not under a witch's spell. But, if that is the case, what was the cause of the girls' symptoms? There are several theories.

One theory is that the afflictions were caused by eating rye bread that had been infected by a fungus known as ergot. This fungus contains chemicals similar to those used in the hallucinogenic drug LSD and causes a variety of symptoms that can be consistent with those alleged to be afflicted by witchcraft.

Other medical conditions have been seen as possibilities as well, such as encephalitis and Lyme disease. Even post-traumatic stress disorder has been considered as a possibility, caused by the stress the girls suffered during King William's War.

Hysteria is yet another theory. Chadwick Hansen argues that the girls suffered from hysteria caused by the *fear* of witchcraft, and not actual witchcraft itself. The girls, who had grown up hear-

Two events particularly intrigued Mather. The first involved an invisible chain. Mather described how "they" would chain Martha up and pull her from her seat toward the fire. When Mather stomped on the hearth, Martha would scream out at him that he jarred the chain and hurt her back. And on one memorable day he personally defended her from the invisible chains, claiming in *Memorable Providences* that "Once I did with my own hand knock it off as it began to be fastened about her."

The demons tormenting Martha also brought her an invisible horse, according to Mather: "Upon this would she give a Spring as

ing stories about witches, worried about being bewitched themselves and experienced symptoms that were, literally, all in their
heads. If someone believes strongly enough in witchcraft, it is an
easy step to believe that one *has* been bewitched. Indeed, many
of the girls' symptoms, including what appeared to be bite marks
and an urge to throw themselves into fires, are classic signs of
hysteria.

Yet another possibility is what is known as projection. Given
that the accused were primarily women between the ages of
41 and 60, and the afflicted girls were mostly adolescents, it
is not unlikely that the teenage girls, chafing under the strict
rules of the Puritans, projected their anger outward in the form
of fits and verbal attacks against those who they saw as their
oppressors.

The truth behind what caused the outbreak of "witchcraft"
in Puritan New England may never be known with absolute certainty. Whatever the reason, though, it is obvious that there are
logical, scientific reasons for the girls' symptoms.

one mounting on a Horse, and Settling herself in a Riding Posture—
she would in her Chair be agitated as one sometimes Ambling, sometimes Trotting, and sometimes Galloping very furiously."

Cotton Mather was fascinated by the working of what he called
"the invisible world," and devoted much time to the family. Attempts
to "cure" the Goodwin children of their "possession" were at first
futile. Finally, according to Mather, on November 27, 1688, "the
power of the Enemy was broken"; the attacks became less and less
violent until life finally returned to normal for the Goodwin family.
The "possession" of the children had ended.

The next year, Cotton Mather published *Memorable Providences, Relating to Witchcrafts and Possessions*, in which he described the events of the preceding summer and fall. The book was a major success and established him as an "expert" on the "workings of the invisible world"—so much so in fact that eighteen months after his book first appeared, when other young girls began to show signs of bewitchment, thoughts turned to Cotton Mather. According to the minister John Hale, as quoted in Kenneth Silverman's *The Life and Times of Cotton Mather*, the new cases were "in all things afflicted as bad as John Goodwin's children at Boston, in the year 1689. So that he that will read Mr. Mather's Book of *Memorable Providences*, page 3 etc., may Read part of what these Children, and afterward sundry grown persons suffered by the hand of Satan, at Salem Village, and parts adjacent."

In other words, it was Cotton Mather whose book was one of the driving forces behind the infamous Salem witch trials. It was Cotton Mather who helped to teach New Englanders to see witchcraft all around them. And by "teaching" New England about witchcraft and the need to fight against it, hundreds of innocent people were arrested and charged with witchcraft. Twenty-nine people, both men and women, were hanged for their supposed crimes.

AN INFLUENTIAL FIGURE

Today most people believe that there is no such thing as possession. But to Cotton Mather and most of his fellow Puritans, the evidence for the reality of witches was obvious—witches, Satan, and evil temptations lurked everywhere, and it was up to man to fight against them. Unfortunately for Mather, it is this same belief in witchcraft and his controversial role in the Salem witch trials that is what he is best remembered for today. Indeed, Mather, one of the most prominent and influential men of his time has, with the exception of his involvement in the Salem witch trials, largely faded from the American memory.

During his lifetime, though, he was a towering intellectual figure, one of the most important men of his age. Six days after his death on February 13, 1728, the *New-England Weekly Journal* paid tribute to him by saying,

> He was perhaps the *principal Ornament* of this Country, and the greatest *Scholar* that was ever bred in it. But besides his universal Learning; his exalted Piety and extensive *Charity*, his entertaining *Wit*, and singular *Goodness of Temper* recommended him to all, that were Judges of real and distinguishing merit.

Today of course, all that is forgotten. But there *is* much more to Cotton Mather than the public image of a stern-faced religious fanatic, frantically trying to stomp out witchcraft that didn't exist.

He was the most prominent minister of his time, one whose sermons influenced generations of religious believers. He was an extraordinarily prolific writer. He was involved in politics and science. He was married three times and was the father of fifteen children. His life allows us a view of a turbulent period in American history, during which the strict religious beliefs of the early Puritan settlers began to be challenged by a more secular, worldly view of society.

But to understand the life and times of Cotton Mather, we are going to have to go back a few years before he was born, to the Great Migration and the arrival of the Puritans in America. We're going to have to explore a mindset far different than our own, one with beliefs and ideas on how to live one's life that are perhaps as alien to us as we can possibly imagine. But, unless we're able to understand what the Puritans thought and believed, we will never be able to understand why Cotton Mather thought what he thought, did what he did, and lived the life that he lived.

2

The Puritans

It was the British novelist L.P. Hartley who famously said in his novel *The Go-Between*, "The past is a foreign country: they do things differently there." In other words, it is easy to fall into the habit of thinking about people in the past—be they Romans during the age of Julius Caesar, Americans during the time of the Civil War, or the French under King Louis XVI—as being pretty much the same as us. Except, of course, for speaking differently than we do and wearing odd clothes. This couldn't be farther from the truth.

The past *is* a foreign country. It *is* different, and so were the people. They way they thought, the things they believed, the way they saw and perceived the world around them, the way they approached and lived their lives *were* very different than they are today. And the way the Puritans saw and defined their world and their own particular sense of mission in America was no exception.

WHERE THEY CAME FROM

Originally, the Puritans were members of various Protestant groups that opposed the beliefs and rituals of the Church of England under King James I (1566–1625). (The Protestants came into being as opponents to the Roman Catholic Church. The Church of England is considered a Protestant denomination, but many aspects of its laws and teachings as well as its worship services are based on Roman Catholicism.) The Puritans strongly condemned the Church of England's use of religious icons, such as pictures and statues, written prayers, instrumental music, and other elements of religious services.

While the Puritans felt that their own observances were an attempt to get closer to what God wanted from man, to some non-Puritans they came across as troublesome, overly religious people trying to interfere with the rights of others to practice their religion as *they* felt was right. Both James I and his successor, Charles I (1600–1649), were angered by their strict religious beliefs and forced them to leave England. After living in other nearby European countries such as the Netherlands, the Puritans began leaving for New England.

The first to depart are known today by Americans as the Pilgrims, the same Pilgrims who founded the Plymouth colony in Massachusetts with the hope of establishing God's Kingdom on Earth and who gave us Thanksgiving. Nine years later another group of Puritans was given a charter, a form of government deed, granting them permission to start their own colony, the nearby Massachusetts Bay Colony.

This larger migration, known as the Great Migration, began with the Winthrop Fleet of 1630 (named for governor of the Massachusetts Bay Colony John Winthrop), whose 11 ships delivered 700

The Puritans disagreed with the Church of England's use of religious icons and routinely damaged such symbols. Above, a figure of a saint with its face scratched out.

passengers to the Massachusetts Bay Colony. This migration continued until 1640. With the outbreak of the English Civil War in
1641, some recent immigrants returned to England to fight on the
Puritan side, and many who had planned to leave didn't, since the
ultimate victor, Oliver Cromwell, was himself a Puritan.

From 1630 through 1640, nearly 20,000 Puritans immigrated to
New England. Those numbers were far lower than the number of
English citizens who immigrated to Ireland, Canada, and the Caribbean during this time. But then, *those* migrations were motivated by
economical profit and tended to consist nearly entirely of men. The
Great Migration was called the Great Migration not because of sheer
numbers, but because of the purpose of the endeavor. Entire Puritan
families migrated, families who were well educated and left relatively
prosperous lives with the purpose of establishing a new society, based
on religious values, in the New World.

John Winthrop, in his sermon "A Model of Christian Charity,"
laid out the basis for the new colony, telling the colonists that their
new community would be a "city upon a hill," watched by the entire
world:

> For we must consider that we shall be as a city upon a hill. The
> eyes of all people are upon us. So that if we shall deal falsely
> with our God in this work we have undertaken . . . we shall
> be made a story and a by-word throughout the world. We
> shall open the mouths of enemies to speak evil of the ways
> of God . . . We shall shame the faces of many of God's wor-
> thy servants, and cause their prayers to be turned into curses
> upon us til we be consumed out of the good land whither we
> are-a-going.

Winthrop believed, as did other Puritans, that all nations had
a covenant with God. But, since England had violated its covenant

because of the errors of the Church of England, the Puritans had to leave their homes and begin again. Winthrop claimed that the Puritans had created a new, special agreement with God, similar to that between God and the people of Israel. Further, he believed that by building a community based on purified Christianity in the New World, his followers would serve as an example to the Old World they had left behind for building a model Protestant community.

This model Puritan community was not a place that valued or even thought of freedom in the same way that we do today. While the Puritans wanted the freedom to practice their own religion, that freedom did not extend toward other religions. Since they were convinced that theirs was the only true religion, they forced everyone in the Massachusetts Bay Colony to follow the dictates of their puritanical faith, even if they were not Puritans.

Indeed, since the Puritans saw themselves as God's chosen people, they believed they had been sent to the New World to fight a battle against the devil, who they saw as the source of all evil. Because of this, they viewed Native Americans, European settlers of other faiths, and even some unexplained forces of nature to be forms of the devil himself, and therefore direct challenges to the will of God.

Many believed that prior to the birth of Christ, the devil had brought the Native Americans to the New World as his own chosen people, isolating them on the continent to keep them from learning the word of the Gospels. Thus, many Puritans saw America as truly the land of the devil. By building churches and bringing the word of the Gospel to the devil's own land, New England became, according to Cotton Mather himself, as quoted by Kenneth Silverman, "a vexing *Eyesore*," to the devil, who tried every way possible to "undermine his plantation and force us out of our Country."

To fight the fight against the devil, the Puritans, as soldiers in the battle between good and evil, established a highly structured society with rigid laws and rules based on the Bible. Any sinful act was seen

NATHANIEL HAWTHORNE

For many readers of American literature, the works of Nathaniel Hawthorne (July 4, 1804–May 19, 1864) are their introduction to the world of Puritan New England. In many of his novels and short stories, Hawthorne brings that era to life, telling tales that suggest to the reader that guilt, sin, and evil are all natural qualities of humanity.

Perhaps his best-known work is the novel *The Scarlet Letter* (1850), which tells the story of Hester Prynne, a young woman living in seventeenth-century Boston. He opens the novel with a scene of excruciating power: Hester being led from the town prison with her infant daughter in her arms. On her gown is an uppercase letter *A*, a letter that represents the act of adultery that she has committed and is to be a symbol of her sin. It is a badge of shame for all to see.

The book tells her story, as well as that of her elderly husband, Roger Chillingworth, and her lover, the Reverend Arthur Dimmesdale. By exploring the guilt, sin, and love that bind the three major characters, Hawthorne draws an unforgettable portrait of Hester's struggle to create a new life for herself and her daughter, Pearl.

as treason against both God and the community and as an invitation to the devil.

The Puritans also believed that all humans were essentially sinners and had been ever since Adam's fall in the Garden of Eden. It was only through a continuous effort to achieve God's grace that one's soul could be saved. It was a paradox that author Robert Middlekauff noted in his book *The Mathers: Three Generations of Puritan Intellectuals*:

The creed the community lived by, the ministers that preached to it, the books and tracts that came from its presses, all told the Puritan "you are helplessly and hopelessly sunk in sin, your will is corrupt, your understanding impaired, your emotions base, but though only God can save you, you must strive after the grace that will bring eternal peace, you must exert yourself to all your capacity."

PURITAN SOCIETY

It is a concept that can be difficult for us to understand, but for the Puritan, it was everyday reality. This led, as Middlekauff pointed out, to the familiar figure of the Puritan, "the tormented soul, constantly examining his every thought and action, now convinced that hell awaits him, now lunging after the straw of hope that he is saved, and then once more falling into despair. He wants to believe, he tries, he fails, he succeeds, he fails—always on the cycle of alternating moods."

To avoid the possibility of transgression (an act in violation of a law), the church held tight control over every aspect of daily life. Any activities that might open the door to sin, such as games, dancing, frequent bathing, physical recreation, and social gatherings outside of church, were strictly prohibited. Because the community was so closely knit and united against any possible "evil," *anyone* who deviated from the rules, *anyone* who was in the slightest way "different," aroused immediate suspicion. Indeed, Puritans were often disturbed by any signs of difference, which they interpreted as the presence of evil in their midst. For example, they thought crippled, aged, poor, eccentric, deformed, and even sickly people were quite possibly the offspring of Satan.

Puritan laws gave women as little freedom and power as possible. For example, a widow who tried to keep her dead husband's estate rather than pass it onto her sons was in danger of losing everything in court. An adulteress could be put to death for her crime. Puritans believed that women could gain access to power only through communion with the devil. Because of this belief about the role of women, strong-willed, independent, and unmarried women were the ones most frequently accused of witchcraft.

On all levels of society, it was men who held the reins of power. Husbands had authority over their wives, fathers had authority over their children, and masters held power over the servants in the family. The family itself was the basic unit of society. It was the place where Puritans learned religious, ethical, and social values and the expectations of the community. The English Puritan William Gouge wrote in his tract *Of Domestical Duties*, "a family is a little Church, and a little Commonwealth . . . it is a school where in the first principles and grounds of government and subjection are learned."

In the Puritan family, authority and obedience characterized the relationship between parents and children. To love one's children meant to discipline them. Disciplining disobedient children, like most actions, arose from a spiritual concern: A breakdown in family rule symbolized a breakdown in God's own order. Puritan Richard Greenham wrote that parents have disobedient children because they themselves have been disobedient children to the Lord. Nothing was more important to the Puritans than obedience to one's superiors, to one's parents, and to the Lord.

Yet at the same time, despite the intensity of their religious beliefs and superstitions, a high value was placed on education. The leaders of the original colony had seen themselves as part of an international world of scholars. They had attended top schools such as Oxford and Cambridge and maintained communications with intellectuals from all over Europe. Indeed, within six months after the first large migrations, colony leaders had founded Harvard College.

New England Puritans arrest an old woman accused of witchcraft in the seventeenth century.

By the 1670s, all New England colonies (with the exception of Rhode Island), had passed legislation that established mandatory literacy for children. In 1647, Massachusetts passed a law that required towns to hire a schoolmaster to teach writing. Different forms of schooling quickly emerged, ranging from the "dame" or "reading" school, a form of instruction conducted by women in their homes for small children, to "Latin, or grammar," schools for boys already literate in English and ready to move on to the study of grammar in Latin, Hebrew, and Greek.

Reading schools would often be the only source of education for girls, while boys would leave those schools to move on to the town grammar schools. It was the women's job to introduce all children to reading; men taught boys everything beyond that. Since girls were forbidden to play any role in the ministry, and since grammar schools were designed to prepare boys for university, Latin grammar schools did not admit women. (Neither did Harvard.)

Why did the Puritans place such an importance on literacy? In order for Puritans to become holy, to be able to achieve the necessary state of Grace, they needed to be able to read the Bible. As the articles of faith of 1549 boldly stated, "Holy Scripture containeth all things necessary to salvation." So although reading the Bible did not necessarily guarantee one's salvation, it laid the groundwork, and it was the duty of every good Puritan to search out scriptural truth for him- or herself.

The other reason for mandating literacy was the concern that children who didn't learn to read would grow "barbarous." In addition, children needed to be able to read in order to "understand . . . the capital laws of this country," as Massachusetts law declared. In every aspect of life, order was of the utmost importance to the Puritan community, a group trying both to build a home in a wilderness and create a perfected community from scratch.

3

Three Generations of Mathers

Three generations of Mather men were among the Puritan world's most prominent clergymen and religious thinkers. The founder of the dynasty, and the man who first settled in New England was Richard Mather (1596–1669).

Richard Mather was born in Lowton, in the parish of Winwick, near Liverpool, England. His family, while poor, was of high enough status that they were entitled to bear a coat of arms. After years in school both studying and teaching, he began his preaching career in November 1618 at Toxteth, where he was ordained in early 1619.

In August through November 1633 he was suspended for nonconformity in matters of ceremony; as a "nonconformist," or Puritan, he refused to perform the elaborate rituals of the Church of England. He was suspended again in 1634 when Richard Neile, the Archbishop of York, learned that he had never worn a surplice (the long robe worn over the cassock) during the 15 years of his ministry.

Mather had earned a fine reputation as a preacher in and about Liverpool. But, advised by letters from John Cotton and Thomas Hooker, two Puritan clergymen who had already made the Great Migration, in May 1635 he joined a company of pilgrims and embarked at Bristol for New England. He arrived in Boston on August 15, 1635, and, moving on to Dorchester, Connecticut, he became the town's pastor until his death in 1669.

He was an accomplished preacher, described in one biography as "aiming to shoot his arrows not over his people's heads, but into their Hearts and Consciences." He was a leader of New England Congregationalism (a system of church government in which every church is independent and not under the rule of a larger church hierarchy) and a prolific writer, best known for writing (along with Thomas Welde and John Eliot) the "Bay Psalm Book." This book, whose full title is *The Whole Booke of Psalmes Faithfully Translated into English Metre* (1640), translated the biblical Psalms into English meter and was probably the first book printed in the English colonies.

He fathered six sons with his first wife, Katherine Hoult (or Holt), four of whom became ministers. The most famous of these was his youngest son, Increase Mather, who became the most prominent religious leader of his generation. (Richard's second wife was Sarah Hankredge, the widow of John Cotton, the clergyman who had preached the farewell sermon to John Winthrop's historic fleet in 1630, one of the very men who had urged him to come to the New World.)

Born on June 21, 1639, in Dorchester, Massachusetts, Increase was given his unusual first name by his father because of "the never-to-be-forgotten *Increase*, of every sort, wherewith God favoured the

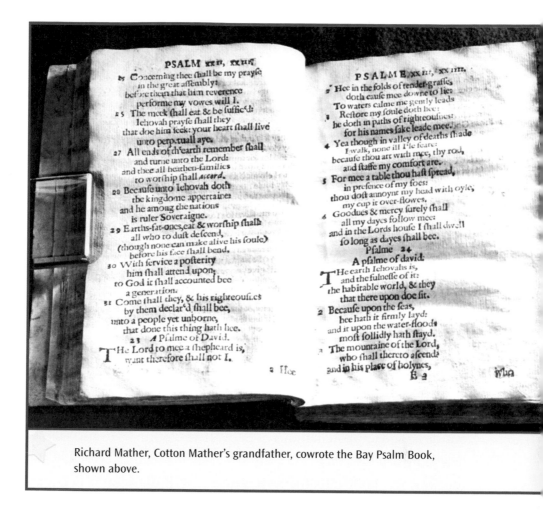

Richard Mather, Cotton Mather's grandfather, cowrote the Bay Psalm Book, shown above.

country, about the time of his Nativity." Like many, Increase received his early education at home from his parents, and, very much his father's son, showed a decided inclination for learning and religious study.

At the age of 12, Increase entered Harvard, where he studied under John Norton, a noted Puritan divine (someone well versed in theology). When he graduated in 1656 with a bachelor of arts degree, he began to train for the ministry. He gave his first sermon on his eighteenth birthday. Soon thereafter, he preached at his father's church. One month later, he set sail for England, where he visited his older brother Samuel, who was a Puritan minister in Ireland, and received further education at Trinity College in Dublin, where he received a master of arts degree.

Increase returned to Massachusetts in 1661, where he married Maria Cotton, who was, in fact, his stepsister because of his father's marriage to Sarah Hankredge, the widow of John Cotton. Sarah was Maria's mother. Known for his simple preaching style and splendid voice, Increase was ordained as minister of the North Church (the original Old North Meetinghouse, not to be confused with the Anglican/Episcopal Old North Church, made famous by the midnight ride of Paul Revere). His leadership of the church, whose congregation included many of Boston's upper class and governing class, made him one of the most influential people in the colony, both religiously and politically.

As such, he was a strict Puritan, opposing anything he saw as contradictory to or distracting from his religious beliefs. He supported official suppression of drunkenness, unnecessary effort on Sundays, and any ostentatious or decorative clothing. He also wholeheartedly believed that God's disfavor was revealed in everyday life: the weather, political situations, attacks by Indians, and fires and floods were all signs of God's displeasure.

And yet, Increase was also a man of great learning: an author of more than 125 published books, a scholar who, as cited by Kenneth Silverman, once said that he "loved to be in no place on the Earth, so much as in my Study." He would begin working there by seven in the morning and was often still there at midnight, only leaving for meals or to supervise religious instruction and devotion by his family. As Silverman notes, a contemporary wrote, "He love'd this *Study* to a kind of excess, and in a manner *liv'd* in it from his Youth to a great Old Age."

The study where Increase Mather spent so much of his life was in the house that he and Maria had lived in from the time they were married. It had been the home of Maria's father, the Puritan preacher John Cotton, and was located no more than a 15-minute walk from Boston's Town Hall. Even though Boston was, in 1663, the largest town in North America, with a population of about 3,000 inhabitants, it was still largely rural. The Mather home stood on nearly an acre and a half (0.6 hectares) of fenced-in land, with a garden and orchard that allowed the couple to grow their own fruit and vegetables.

It was in this house that Cotton Mather was born on February 12, 1663. Increase, as quoted by Kenneth Silverman, named his first-born son after his wife's father, "the most Eminent Man of God that ever *New-England* saw." The son of one clergyman, the grandson of two clergymen, and the nephew of five clergymen, Cotton Mather's future was largely settled from the moment he was born.

EARLY CHILDHOOD

Indeed, early in his son's life, Increase, who felt he had the gift of prophecy (as well as a never-ending conviction that because of his failings as God's servant his death was imminent), had an unshakeable conviction that his son had been chosen. He is quoted by Kenneth Silverman as writing that, "If ever Father had a particular Faith for a child, then I had so for that child, of whom I could with Assurance say, God has blessed him, yea, and He shall be blessed."

Young Cotton did what he could to live up to his father's convictions. By his own telling, he learned to write before he went to school and began to pray as soon as he began to speak. But as a bonus, he wasn't repeating the standard prayers he was hearing from his parents. He was inventing prayers for himself.

It seems likely that Increase practiced at home as a parent what he preached to his congregation. He believed that parents should spend as much time as possible educating both their children's minds and hearts; they should fervently pray for their acceptance of God's grace or conversion. He also believed that parents should explain to their children from a very young age that by their very nature they are sinful and corrupt, and, finally, to let them know their greatest responsibility is, as Silverman notes "to know and serve the God of their Father."

There were problems, though, early in Cotton's life. Increase Mather, shaken by his own father's death in 1669, experienced a year of ill health, depression, and what he called "Ephilates," nightmares so severe that he felt he was being tested by Satan. Having horrible dreams every night deprived him of sleep and made him question whether his faith that God would ease his suffering was nothing but a delusion. Although the nightly round of nightmares ended by the fall of 1671, Increase suffered horrifying nightmares for the rest of his life.

At around the same time, the family moved into a larger residence, just blocks from the North Church, which actually owned the house. By this time, Cotton was one of five children; his siblings were Maria (born March 1665), Elizabeth (January 1667), Nathaniel (July 1669), and Sarah (November 1671). The new large family added financial pressures to Increase's growing resentment toward a church and congregation that he felt did not appreciate him. He began to fantasize about leaving his congregation behind, cited by Silverman as writing that, "When I am gone, my poor people will believe that the grief which I sustained by their neglects of me and mine, was unprofitable for them."

It seems unlikely, though, that the young Cotton knew of his father's inner turmoil. He was busy living a life of piety and

Increase Mather was a strict Puritan and a scholar. As an influential member of the Boston community, Mather became involved in the Salem witch trials and preached sermons calling for level heads.

BOSTON LATIN SCHOOL

Cotton Mather was not the only famous graduate of Boston Latin School. Since its founding in 1635, many famous Americans have received their education at what is known as the oldest existing school in the United States.

While Boston Latin's first class included fewer than ten students, the school now has 2,400 pupils drawn from all parts of Boston. Among its illustrious graduates are four Harvard presidents, four Massachusetts governors, four signers of the Declaration of Independence (Samuel Adams, John Hancock, William Hooper, and Robert Treat Paine; one additional signer, Benjamin Franklin, attended Boston Latin but failed to graduate), art historian Bernard Berenson, conductor and composer Leonard Bernstein, essayist Ralph Waldo Emerson, jazz critic and historian Nat Hentoff, philosopher George Santayana, and counterterrorism expert Richard A. Clarke.

learning, fervently studying the Bible, never less than 15 chapters per day, divided into morning, afternoon, and evening exercises. He also began to emulate his father by composing prayers for his classmates and, as Silverman notes, urging them to better behavior, "[rebuking] my Play-mates, for their Wicked *Words* and *Ways.*"

As a result, as Silverman points out, seven- or eight-year-old Cotton learned a valuable lesson. Being a Mather often meant experiencing ingratitude because his classmates did not always appreciate Cotton's concern for how they lived their lives and for the condition of their souls. "Sometimes I suffered from them, the persecution of not only *Scoffs*," he recalled," but *Blows* often, for my Rebukes." Not surprisingly, Increase Mather, who often felt unappreciated himself, was proud of his son's early attempts to improve men's souls.

Cotton was equally his father's son when it came to intelligence and love of learning. After being taught at home and then in a "dame" school, Cotton attended the prestigious Boston Latin School, a public exam school founded in 1635 that even today is considered to be one of the top high schools in the country. There, his instructor was the famous Ezekiel Cheever, America's first great schoolteacher. Cheever noted that while he often was forced to beat his students, Cotton never required such punishment.

Cotton's father, as quoted by Kenneth Silverman, considered him to be "Tender and Weakly" and often kept him home from school to study, so it is difficult to determine how much of his education he received from his father and how much from Ezekiel Cheever. Nonetheless, it is known that by the age of 11 he had read in Latin the Roman writers Cato, Tully, Ovid, and Virgil; had read most of the New Testament in Greek; had read Homer; and had begun the study of Hebrew grammar. It is said that he spoke Latin so well that not only could he write out the notes of sermons as the preacher spoke them in church, but he could even write them in Latin while the preacher spoke in English!

Incredible as it may seem, by 1674, at the age of just 11 and a half, Cotton Mather had passed the entrance exams for Harvard College and was admitted as a student, the youngest in its history. It was obvious to all who knew him that Cotton was destined for an illustrious career as a clergyman and scholar, but there was one problem. Cotton had developed a handicap that threatened to keep him out of the pulpit before his career had even begun.

4

His Father's Son

What was this handicap that threatened Cotton Mather's career before it had even started? Sometime in the late summer or fall of 1674 (Increase Mather first made note of it in October 1674, just a few months into his son's freshman year at Harvard), Cotton Mather, whose livelihood depended on his ability to preach to a congregation, developed a stammer.

Father and son both knew what such a speech impediment could mean. As quoted by Kenneth Silverman, in his diary Increase Mather worried "lest the Hesitancy in his speech should make him uncapable of improvement in the work of the ministry, whereunto I had designed him." Cotton himself wrote years later that the stammer made his likely career "a Thing as much despaired of, as anything in the World." Having a stammer was obviously a humiliation for Cotton, who often wrote in his later years about the pain and embarrassment suffered by stutterers.

According to his diary, on October 7, 1674, Increase and his wife called Cotton into his study, where the three of them prayed together, and as quoted by Silverman, with "many Tears bewailed our sinfulness, and begged of God mercy in this particular." And, although Increase vowed to trust in God to work his will, help came to his son via more earthly means.

Cotton received a visit to his rooms at Harvard from Elijah Corlet, a well-known, elderly schoolmaster. Corlet, as quoted by Silverman, told him "*My Friend*, I now Visit you for nothing, but only to Talk with you about the *Infirmity* in your *Speech*, and offer you my Advice about it; Because I suppose tis a Thing that greatly Trouble [sic] you." The course of treatment that Corlet suggested to Cotton was surprising.

Corlet pointed out to Cotton that in his experience, nobody ever stuttered or stammered while singing psalms. His advice? Cotton should speak slowly and deliberately and drawl his words out *almost* as if he was singing. He then demonstrated by reciting to Cotton the first verse in Homer and dragging out every syllable. While drawling out his words might not be ideal, he admitted, it was certainly better than stammering.

And, by slowing down his speech, it would give him time to think slowly and find a word that would be easier to say than one that was difficult to speak without stuttering. The suggestion worked. By using Corlet's method, Cotton got used to speaking correctly, and he was gradually able to speak at a more normal pace. The stammer, however, never completely went away, and until the day he died Cotton remained conscious of the need to avoid speaking too quickly.

PROPHECIES COMING TRUE?

While his son studied at Harvard, Increase Mather continued to receive "intimations" from God, intimations that often came true.

The colonial village of Brookfield, Massachusetts, is burned by Native Americans during King Phillip's War. Increase Mather believed he had received signs from God that such an event would occur.

Early in the year 1674, Increase Mather received signs from God that he would soon strike New England by sword. Never content to keep this information to himself, and believing that God had informed him so that he could be his messenger, Increase preached two sermons to his congregation from the biblical book of Ezekiel 7:7: The day of Trouble is near. One year later, in the summer of 1675, King Phillip's War began. Whole towns were destroyed; large numbers of Native Americans were left dead; and in Boston itself, it was estimated that nearly every person had lost a relation or friend to the war.

Cotton and Increase often prayed together to bring an end to the war. On one special day Increase begged God to destroy the Native American leader King Phillip. In "less than a Week, after This," Cotton recalled, as quoted by Silverman, "*the Thing was Accomplished.*" King Phillip was shot and quartered; the city of Boston was presented with his hands, Plymouth was given his head.

There was yet another prophecy to come true. Shortly after the end of the war, Increase Mather became possessed with the fear that Boston would be punished by God with fire. On November 19, 1676, he again preached a sermon warning his congregation of what he was certain was about to happen. Not surprisingly, many of his congregants seemed skeptical about his prophecy, and Increase spent many hours pacing the floors of his study, bewailing their lack of faith.

Increase Mather was frequently the victim of insomnia, so it is not altogether surprising that he was awake very early on the morning of November 27. Increase, however, as quoted by Kenneth Silverman, attributed it to providence: "God (and I believe his Angels) did so influence that I could not sleep that morning." He was awake to smell the smoke from the fire that destroyed a good part of Boston. Although Increase was able to save his family and most of his 1,000-volume library, his house, most of his other belongings, and the North Church were destroyed. (Within a year, the North Church was rebuilt and the Mather family was living in a new home.)

KING PHILLIP'S WAR

It seems unlikely that the Pilgrims could have survived their first year at Plymouth (1620) without the help of the Wampanoag, a Native American tribe led by their sachem (chief) Massasoit. But by 1675 tensions between colonists and Native Americans had begun to grow. The Wampanoag became more and more dependent on English manufactured goods, which led to the ever-increasing sales of Wampanoag land to pay for those goods. At the same time, the Puritans' consuming interest in converting the Native Americans away from their own beliefs to Christianity added to increasing resentment between the two groups.

In 1675, three tribal members were tried and executed by the English for the murder of a converted Wampanoag. In response, the Wampanoag, now led by Massasoit's son Metacom, known to the colonists as King Phillip, attacked a number of colonial settlements, killing dozens of men, women, and children. Colonial forces responded, destroying native villages and slaughtering their inhabitants. Soon other Native American tribes, including

GRADUATION

Despite the struggle with his stammer, the turmoil of King Phillip's War, and the destruction of a good part of the city of Boston by fire, Cotton Mather's education proceeded largely uninterrupted. Harvard's curriculum was intended to educate men in literature, the arts, and sciences, and included courses in Greek, Hebrew, logic, ethics, metaphysics, mathematics, rhetoric, oratory, and theology. Cotton excelled at it all.

By the time he was 14 years old, Cotton was writing in Hebrew and had completed the full curriculum before finishing his junior year. He had also composed systems of logic and physics that were the Narragansett, joined the battle, and the entire region fell into conflict.

The tide turned against the Native Americans in April 1676, when, low on supplies, the Narragansett were defeated and their chief, Canochet, was killed. Four months later, King Phillip was betrayed by a raiding party of Native Americans friendly to the colonists and was also killed. His head was placed on a stake and paraded throughout Plymouth Colony, his son was sold into slavery, and many other captives were forced into servitude throughout the New England colonies. With that, King Phillip's War was over.

The cost to both sides was enormous. More than 600 colonists and 3,000 Native Americans had been killed, and it would be more than 20 years before all of the devastated frontier settlements could be reoccupied. For the New England Native Americans it was an end to the civilization they had known. Their population had been decimated to the point where their impact on further colonial development was non-existent.

being used by other students. He had also read hundreds of books, and for a time, became so interested in science that, while still suffering from his stammer, he seriously considered becoming a physician. Even though that soon passed, another crisis was soon to follow.

Often ill and painfully thin, Cotton, in a way similar to his father, became convinced that he was destined to die young. With that fear came periods of religious doubt, certain that because of what he saw as his own sinful vileness, he was unacceptable to God. He admitted these fears to his father, who reassured him that no sinner who sincerely repented would be turned away by Christ.

Soon after, while praying, Cotton found himself certain that Christ had accepted him. As cited by Silverman, he wrote that, "I sensibly felt an unaccountable *Cloud* and *Load* go off my spirit, and from that Minute I was much altered, by a New *Light*, and *Life*, and *Ease* arriving to me, as the Sunrise does change the World, from the Condition of *Midnight*."

With that resolved, Cotton delved deeper into the religious life. In 1676 he began making detailed notes on the sermons he heard. The next year, he began serving as his father's private secretary, copying documents by hand into the official church records. He also began to observe entire days of private prayers and fasting. Like his father, his life was beginning to wholly revolve around the church and the state of his own soul.

In 1678, at the age of just 15, Cotton Mather graduated from Harvard. At the commencement ceremonies, Urian Oakes, the president of Harvard, singled him out for praise, reminding the assembled audience of the illustrious heritage Cotton had to live up to.

> Mather is named Cotton Mather. What a name! I beg pardon, Gentlemen, I should have said what Names! . . . If he brings back and represents the Piety, the Erudition, the elegant Ability, the Sound Sense, the Prudence, and the Dignity of his Grandfathers . . . he may be said to have gained success; nor do I lack hope but that in this youth Cotton and Mather in fact as well as in name will unite and live again.
>
> —Norma Jean Lutz, *Cotton Mather: Author,*
> *Clergyman, and Scholar*

Imagine being just 15 years old, a graduate of Harvard, and living with that kind of pressure.

GETTING STARTED

Cotton Mather began his career as a preacher by acknowledging his family heritage. He preached his first public sermon on August 22, 1680, at his grandfather Richard Mather's church in Dorchester. The following Sunday he preached for his father in Boston, and the Sunday after that he preached in the Boston church once led by his grandfather John Cotton.

The initial response to his preaching was positive. The men of his father's congregation voted to have Cotton hired as his father's assistant in preaching. In addition, he was offered a job in New Haven, Connecticut, and letters came from as far away as England and Ireland as word spread throughout the Puritan community about the Mather family's bright new star.

Curiously, Increase Mather opposed his son's joining him in the ministry of the North Church and even encouraged him to accept the position in New Haven. Perhaps Increase was jealous of his son's talents. It also is possible that because Increase felt underappreciated and mistreated by his congregation, he was angered by their seeming enthusiasm for his son. It is even possible that he was eager to avoid any possibility of nepotism, the idea that Cotton had received the offer *because* of his father. Whatever the real reason may have been, it would be another five years before Cotton became fully ordained.

Cotton Mather spent much of those five years in grueling, unrelenting self-examination. He questioned his ability to receive God's grace and proceeded to identify his sins and punish himself for them. He would spend hours, even days, lying on the floor of his study, distressed beyond belief over his perceived sins of laziness, lust, and pride. According to Silverman, he wrote, "Lord, Wherewithall shall a young man cleanse his way . . . I have certainly been one of the filthiest Creatures upon Earth."

Pride, in particular, was the sin he found most difficult to cleanse himself of. He wanted to be, as quoted by Silverman, what his father had been, "a Young Man every where admired, and Applauded, and Accepted, and Flock'd after." Yet, he also recognized that the very ambition to become a famous preacher stood in opposition to his obligation to glorify not himself, but God.

These sins, real or exaggerated, plagued Cotton, who, as quoted by Silverman, described himself in his diary as a "poor, broken, sorry despicable Vessel," a sinner who was nothing more than "feeble and worthless," "*unsavory Salt,* fit for nothing but the Dunghill," and worthy of nothing more than "Death, Death, Death, forever."

Periods of certainty that God had forgiven him and had chosen him to be his instrument alternated with periods when Cotton felt abandoned by God, uncertain that his own repentance of his sins was real. This was, as mentioned earlier, a common occurrence among Puritans. But Cotton was certain that because of his talents, and because he was attempting to serve God more ardently than others, he felt God's abandonment all the more. (This of course, would lead him to question his pride, and the same cycle would start all over again.)

Cotton developed a series of prayers and actions all designed to bring himself even closer to God. One of these he called "secret prayer," which was a private prayer as opposed to those with the family or in church; Cotton would lock himself in a room alone, begging God to forgive his sins while lying face down on the floor, his mouth in the dust. (We know all of this because of Cotton's diaries, begun in 1681 and kept through 1725. In them, he recorded his prayers, meditations, and religious experiences, with an occasional mention of his domestic life, as well as social and political events. All quotes from his diaries are taken from Kenneth Silverman's biography, *The Life and Times of Cotton Mather*.)

He could never do enough to please God. He tried, before any action, to precede it with the thought "let me do this (or I will do this) for God." He would sing hymns morning and night. Every action, every thought that crossed his mind, was evaluated for worthiness. He met with other young men to pray, hoping that by helping them achieve salvation he was helping himself do the same thing. On one memorable occasion in 1685, after two friends interrupted him during a day-long fast, he invited them to join him, where he entertained them with three sermons, each nearly an hour long!

His goal was to have God in his thoughts every waking moment of every day. He began what he called "Ejaculatory Prayers," a nearly continuous stream of prayers sent up to heaven, based on whatever he was doing or seeing at the moment. He viewed the world from his position as a preacher, "The *Meanest Objects* in the House, or in the Street, have afforded me Thousands of lessons, which I have immediately Sent up to Heaven."

Biographer Kenneth Silverman points out that by transforming his everyday experiences into a glorification of God, he could pray not only in church or with his family, but while eating dinner, while walking down the street, or even just sitting in his study. If, for example, while walking down the street he saw a tall man, he might pray "*Lord*, give that Man, *High Attainments* in Christianity." If he was feeling like someone was ignoring him, he would pray "*Lord*, help that Man, to take a *due notice* of the Lord Jesus Christ."

During the first three years of his candidacy, the severity of his stammer continued to fluctuate. Cotton saw his impediment not as a physical problem or nervous habit but as a punishment by God for his pride. He wrote that "by my early Wickedness and Filthiness, I have provoked Thee, to take away from me one of the greatest Conveniences, enjoyed by thy reasonable Creatures." Not only that, but because he viewed his sins as so severe, he felt that he *deserved* his punishment: "tho' thy *Rod* has been very heavy in this regard upon me . . . Lord, I deserve, not only a *Stammering, Slowness*, but also a total *Dumbness* in my speech."

But, as Cotton Mather and other Puritans understood it, God's punishment was done out of love. By punishing the sinner, God forced the sinner to evaluate himself, become aware of his sins, and then renounce them. The punishment then, was not to make him unhappy, but to bring him closer to God.

Shortly before his twenty-first birthday, Mather felt he had finally conquered his impediment. But the struggle had long-lasting consequences for him psychologically. Because he felt that pride and anger were the underlying causes for the stuttering, he continually strove to present to the world the opposite behavior. Although ambitious, he had to always appear to be selfless. Although often angry, he had to always appear calm and serene. These tensions would appear throughout his life and would lead to problems in the public's perception of him.

But although as a stutterer getting the words out sometimes proved difficult, it seems that Mather never suffered a moment of writer's block. It has been said that he probably wrote as much by hand as anybody *ever* has. Take, for instance, the notebooks he kept at the age of 13, summarizing and evaluating all the sermons he heard. There are *7,000* pages in those notebooks, each with around 250 words per page!

He also, like many in the seventeenth and eighteenth centuries, kept a diary. In it, he was writing not only for himself but for his children to come and for future generations, certain that they could benefit from reading it. The diary is a fascinating (if lengthy) record of one's man life and spiritual journey, complete with a thorough assessment of both his sins and blessings. In one entry written at the age of 20 in 1683, quoted by Norma Jean Lutz in her biography, *Cotton Mather: Author, Clergyman, and Scholar*, he made a list not only of his spiritual blessings (such as his faith and belief in his salvation) but of the "further Favours of God":

1. My improvement in the *Ministry* of the Gospel, after I have been the vilest Creature in the World.

2. The many *Advantages*, which I have to countenance mee, in that Improvement.
   1. The miraculous Freedome of my Speech. [He was now largely free from his stammer.]
   2. A *Library*, exceeding any man's in all this Land.
   3. A desirable *Acceptance*, among the People of God.
   4. An happy *Success* of my Labours, both public and private, Upon Hundreds of Souls.

Of course, although it may sound like it, Cotton Mather did not spend *all* of his time in prayer and self-examination. By 1684, as the older brother to nine younger siblings, he took it upon himself to help with their secular education and to explain their duty to give themselves over to Christ. He also continued his interest in natural history and science, becoming involved with the Boston Philosophical Society.

ORDINATION AND MARRIAGE

In July of 1684, the congregation at North Church once again voted that Cotton Mather become an ordained minister of their church. And, once again, his father, Increase Mather, initially pushed back against their request, but ill and tired, he finally gave in. The date for the ordination was set for Wednesday, May 13, 1685.

Although Cotton had signed a covenant promising to renounce all earthly vanities in favor of service to the Lord, in the days leading up to the ordination he was once again plagued by self-doubt. Uncertain of whether or not he was fit to be a clergyman, on the morning of his ordination he was found in his study, on his knees, praying for an answer. He received it, experiencing, as quoted by Silverman, "a guarantee that he would in his ministry enjoy a mighty presence of the Lord Jesus Christ." His doubts resolved for the moment, he went

At the age of 11, Cotton Mather entered Harvard College, set to follow in the footsteps of his esteemed father and grandfathers.

to the North Church, ready to finally take his official place beside his father.

It has been estimated that nearly half of Boston's population was in attendance. The daylong service began with Cotton offering up an hour and a half of prayers, followed by his preaching a sermon nearly two hours in length. After an extensive sermon from Increase Mather, the official ordination ceremony took place. Cotton received the laying of hands upon his head by his father and two other ministers, and after receiving the "Right Hand of Fellowship" from eighty-year-old minister John Eliot, it was official.

Cotton Mather had been elevated into a partnership with his father in New England's most prestigious and influential church. (Many New England churches were served by two ministers. The "teacher," in this case Increase Mather, stressed matters of doctrine. The "pastor," in this case Cotton Mather, stressed matters of faith.)

He plunged immediately into his work, preaching both at the North Church and at other churches throughout the area. On March 1686 at the North Church, one audience member in particular was the focus of that day's sermon. The man's name was James Morgan. Found guilty of murder and sentenced to be hanged, he had been brought to the sermon to serve as its object, as an example for the rest of the congregation. Cotton used the convicted man as an example of what happens when man gives in to vice and sin and urged the prisoner to turn to Christ before it was too late:

> When the numerous crowd of *Spectators* are, three or four days hence, throng'd about the place where you shall then *breathe your last* before them all, then do you with the heart-piercing *groans of a deadly wounded man* beseech your *Fellow-sinners* that they would *Turn now every one from the evil of his way.*
>
> — From Kenneth Silverman,
> *The Life and Times of Cotton Mather*

When it came time for Morgan to be executed, Cotton was there as well. At the prisoner's request, Cotton accompanied him on his march to the gallows, where they were followed by the thousands who had come to witness the hanging. Cotton's role in the execution added to his prominence, as did the publication of his sermon, entitled *The Call of the Gospel* (1686). The sermon sold so well it went into a second edition, to which the publisher added the manuscript of Cotton's conversation with Morgan on his death march.

Ironically, the success of the sermon led to the first public criticism of Mather's career. As with the rest of his works, Mather's prose style was far from simple; it was lush, involved, and filled with a joy of writing and language. Some critics, however, felt that it was *too* ornate, that it called too much attention to itself. What a writer should aim for, they thought, was the simple direct prose of the Gospels. Mather, while aware that it could be considered a sin, was too proud of his writing style to change it.

His career as a clergyman was taking off, but there was still one more aspect of his life that needed to be filled. To complete his ministry, it was essential for him to marry. As a clergyman, he had an obligation to select a wife who would not only be a companion to him, but serve as a model of good behavior for his congregation and community. With his usual methodical style, it seems that Mather considered several women as his wife, promising God that if he would direct him to the "right" one they would honor him by keeping a private day of Thanksgiving twice a year. He also prayed that God would direct him to a wife with money of her own, to supplement the low salary he earned as a clergyman.

He found the right woman in Abigail Phillips, the daughter of Colonel John Phillips, a well-to-do justice of the peace. He courted her for three months, setting aside one day per week to be spent praying for his success. Either the courtship or the prayer seemed to have been effective, for on May 4, 1686, Cotton Mather, 23 years and three months old, married Abigail Phillips, just one month shy of 16.

The wedding was a major event, attended by many of Boston's most prominent ministers and citizens. The couple began their married life living with Abigail's father, but by the fall of 1686, they had settled into a house in Boston. It was the very house that the Mather family had lived in after the great fire of 1676 had destroyed their first home.

For Cotton Mather, it seemed almost too perfect to be living in the very house in which he had so often prayed. "I could not but observe the Providence of God," he said, as quoted by Silverman, "in ordering my *Comforts* now, in those very Rooms where I had many years before, sought Him with my Prayers." He was happy with his selection of Abigail and thanked God for providing him with "a *Meet-Help*, an extremely desirable Companion for my *Joys* and *Griefs.*"

The new life he was building for himself and his wife, though, would soon be shattered by events both religious and political, events that transformed New England and shaped Cotton Mather's reputation for generations to come.

5

The Salem Witch Trials

For the next 15 years, New England life—political, social, and religious—was in a near constant state of turmoil. For the Puritans, who always considered themselves to be under a constant state of siege, both from the secular world and the invisible world of Satan and his minions, it was a difficult time. It was a period of change, of uncertainty, and of cracks in the once rock-solid Puritan world. And as always, Cotton Mather and his family were in the middle of it all.

The political world of colonial New England was changing. For more than 55 years, the Massachusetts Bay Colony had been governed by a charter granted by the English crown, a charter that allowed the citizens to effectively govern themselves. Attempts had been made by the British government to force the Puritans to return the charter, but they had been ignored. Finally though, England's Catholic king, James II, ordered the charter revoked.

In its place, the king appointed a royal governor, Edmund Andros, who arrived in Boston on December 20, 1686, to govern all of the Dominion of New England. This territory included Massachusetts Bay, Plymouth, New Hampshire, Maine, and the Narragansett Indian country. By 1688 it would include Rhode Island, Connecticut, New York, and the Jerseys as well.

This alone would have been bad enough for the Puritans. But along with the new governor came representatives of the Church of England, the very church that the Puritans had come to the New World to escape. Indeed, Andros ordered that the Congregationalist South Church be used for Anglican services as well. Juries were ordered to admit more non-Congregationalist jurors. In addition, Governor Andros declared that all of the land that the colonists thought they owned was, in fact, owned by the British crown.

Both Increase and Cotton Mather spoke out boldly against the new government, but to no avail. Finally, in desperation, Increase Mather announced that he would go to England to plead the Puritans' case. Governor Andros attempted to keep him from leaving America. But Increase, disguised in a wig and white cloak, boarded a ship bound for England on April 3, 1688. He would be gone for nearly four years, leaving his son in sole charge of his congregation.

Cotton Mather was not only in charge of the North Church, he was also suddenly a leader in the opposition to Governor Andros. Mather was often threatened with arrest and was indeed scheduled to be arrested on April 18, 1689. Instead, armed revolt broke out against the Andros government, and the governor and his supporters were captured.

The extent of Mather's involvement in the actual revolt remains unclear. But his leadership in its aftermath, and in the composition of the publication *Declaration of the Gentlemen*, elaborating on the

Edmund Andros proclaims himself governor of New England in 1686.
Andros's appointment brought the Church of England to New England.

Puritans' grievances against Andros, is unmistakable. He was soon being labeled by his political opponents, according to Silverman, as "the young Pope."

Of course, Mather's time was filled with more than just helping to lead and control a revolt against the colonial government. He had his congregation to think of, now nearly 1,500 members strong. He wrote documents for others, sat on church councils, became a fellow of Harvard College, and even purchased a new house, one where he would live for the next 30 years.

He also had to suffer the loss of his first child, five-month-old Abigail, described by him as being "perhaps One of the Comeliest Infants that have ever been in the world." As a minister, he felt it his responsibility to preach to his congregation on the subject of affliction, telling them that it happens to cause us to question and find out for ourselves why God is punishing us. Yet, in his diary, he acknowledged his personal pain, writing that "few, outward anguishes are equal to these. The dying of a Child is like the tearing of a limb from us."

While his son was contending with political turmoil and personal anguish at home, Increase Mather was facing troubles of his own in England. Each time the crown and government changed, Mather was forced to renegotiate the terms of New England's relationship with the British government. Months of negotiations dragged into years, years that Increase Mather filled with the purchasing of the latest scientific texts and establishing relations with members of the Royal Society of London for Improving Natural Knowledge.

Finally, an agreement was reached. On May 14, 1692, Increase Mather returned to Boston with the new charter and accompanied by the new governor, Sir William Phips. Cotton Mather was pleased with the new governor, with whom he was well acquainted. As quoted by Norma Jean Lutz, he noted in his journal that, "The Governour of the Province is not my Enemy, but one whom I baptized, namely Sir William Phips . . . one of my dearest Friends."

Other Puritans, though, were not so happy. The new charter fell far short of the control over the colony that the Puritans had had under the original charter. The governor, lieutenant governor, and secretary were all to be appointees of the crown. Religious liberty was granted to all colonists (with the exception of Catholics), and the right to vote would no longer be tied to one's religion, but to the owning of property. New England would no longer be an exclusive Puritan stronghold, but the property of the crown.

This shaking of Puritan control over the Massachusetts Bay Colony was reflected in internal turmoil within the colony itself. Earthquakes, fires, and smallpox epidemics were common problems. To the Puritans, these were nothing more than divine punishment for their own internal rot, for the church's loss of control over the state, for a new generation of Puritans who were seen as not as religious as the original settlers.

Within just a short period, the New England Puritans had felt that they and their land had been invaded by such evils as Governor Andros, Native Americans, smallpox, fires, and Anglicans. It is not surprising then that during this time of upheaval, hysteria regarding a new invasion soon swept Massachusetts. As Cotton Mather, quoted by Silverman, wrote, "There is a power of Devils in our Air that are seeking to hurt us." The period of the Salem witch trials was about to begin.

WITCHCRAFT ACCUSATIONS

Of course, the belief in witchcraft was not limited to colonial Massachusetts. During the 1600s, the belief in witchcraft was nearly universal. In Europe, for example, a judge in Bavaria sentenced 274 witches to death in 1629. In the city of Bonn, children as young as three and four years old were accused of having devils for lovers. At Bamberg, a combination witch house and torture chamber was built where 600 witches were said to have been burnt to death over a ten-year period.

Witchcraft cases were also common throughout New England and other areas of the New World. More than 80 such cases were tried between 1647 and 1691, resulting in 20 executions and countless fines, whippings, and banishments. These numbers increased around the time of the Goodwin affair, and even more so after the publication of Cotton Mather's *Memorable Providences, Relating to Witchcrafts and Possessions.*

Numerous sources, for example, reported that the devil appeared to a Cambridge man in 1684, making bird noises. A case in Maine in 1683 involved ringing frying pans, unexplainable arm bites, and floorboards that buckled under the weight of invisible feet. A church deacon in 1684 reported suffering pinpricks from invisible pins and speaking in gibberish. To many, it seemed that the devil was indeed loose in New England.

What was actually going on? The cases reported in New England seem to follow a pattern common among all cases of witchcraft both in America and in Europe. The accuser and the accused almost inevitably knew each other well, usually as neighbors. The accuser had generally suffered an illness, misfortune, or string of bad luck for which there was no apparent explanation. The accuser, though, usually knew that he or she had offended a neighbor in some way and so accused the neighbor of having caused the illness or misfortune in revenge. (The basic thought process would go something like this: I am sick. My neighbor is mad at me. She's a witch who is making me sick.)

The accusers generally suffered from the same symptoms: convulsions, difficulty in speaking, being stuck with (or vomiting up) pins and nails, and seeing visions of cats, pigs, or other animals. And, in both America and in Europe, cases of witchcraft were a "community event." It was always people within the same community who spied on, accused, and gave evidence against one another. Through our modern eyes, accusations of witchcraft seem to be fueled by a combination of misunderstanding, hysteria, and fear of the unknown.

To the Puritans though, belief in witchcraft was not based on superstition; it was based on simple fact. All the turmoil surrounding them, to the Puritan mind, was caused by the devil, in partnership with his earthly servants: witches. To them it was no surprise that the devil would test them by placing witches in their communities. As Cotton Mather wrote in *Wonders of the Invisible World,*

> If any are scandalized that New England, a place of as serious piety as any I can hear of under Heaven should be troubled so much with witches, I think 'tis no wonder: where will the Devil show the most malice but where he is hated, and hateth most?

As the Puritans' life in the New World became more difficult, as their once "shining city on the hill" became more and more a part of the secular British world, it is no wonder that they began to blame "witches" for all of their problems. Eventually, it became clear that eliminating witches was the only way to achieve a lasting victory over the devil.

As John Putnam Demos noted in *Entertaining Satan,* a history of the witchcraft trials,

> Witches could be blamed for a good deal of trouble and difficulty. In this respect the belief in witchcraft was very useful indeed. To discover an unseen hand at work in one's life was to dispel mystery, to explain misfortune, to excuse incompetence.

This print shows a witchcraft trial in Salem. These trials were dramatic events involving hysteria, outbursts, and fainting.

THE TRIALS

Of the many cases of witchcraft reported in New England through-out the seventeenth century, the cases in Salem, Massachu-setts, are by far the most famous. They began in February 1692, in Salem Village, Massachusetts. The Rev. John Hale described the initial outbreak in his account, *A Modest Inquiry*, as quoted by Silverman,

> Mr. Samuel Paris, Pastor of the Church in Salem-Village, had a Daughter of Nine, and a Niece of about Eleven years of Age, sadly Afflicted of they knew not what Distempers; and he

made his application to Physicians, yet still they grew worse; And at length one Physician gave his opinion, that they were under an Evil Hand. This the Neighbours quickly took up, and concluded they were bewitched.

The hysteria quickly spread, and other girls began complaining that they, too, were being molested. They accused three women (or their shapes) as being their tormenters. The three were all "outsiders" in the town: a West Indian slave named Tituba, an elderly woman confined to her bed named "Gammer" Osborne, and a beggar woman named Sarah Good. On February 29, warrants were issued for their arrests on suspicion of witchcraft.

It is interesting to note the questioning and testimony of Sarah Good (as quoted by Kenneth Silverman), given the day after her arrest on March 1. (Good and the rest of the accused were questioned and tried without the benefit of having attorneys.)

Q: Sarah Good, what evil spirit have you familiarity with?

A: None

Q: Have you made no contract with the devil?

Good answered no.

Q: Why do you hurt these children?

A: I do not hurt them. I scorn it.

Q: Who do you employ, then, to do it?

A: I employ nobody.

Q: What creature do you employ then?

A: No creature. But I am falsely accused.

Q: Why did you go away muttering from Mr. Parris's house?

A: I did not mutter, but I thanked him for what he gave my child.

Q: Have you made no contact with the devil?

A: No

H (Judge Hathorne) desired the children, all of them, to look upon her and see if this were the person that had hurt them, and so they did all look upon her and said this was one of the persons that did torment them. Presently they were all tormented.

Q: Sarah Good, do you not see now what you have done? Why do you not tell us the truth? Why do you thus torment these poor Children?

A: I do not torment them.

Q: Who do you employ then?

A: I employ nobody. I scorn it.

Despite Good's denials, other witnesses (including her fellow defendant Tituba) testified that she was, indeed, a witch. Even Good's own husband, William Good, testified that the night before his wife was questioned he saw a wart below her left shoulder that he had never seen before. Given this shocking revelation, it is not surprising that both Good and Tituba were found guilty of the crime of witchcraft. While being held in prison awaiting execution, Good gave birth to her second child, who died in the jail.

In the meantime, accusations of witchcraft in Salem continued to mount. It has been estimated that at one point, nearly 700 people had been accused of witchcraft, and more than 100 accused witches, including Sarah Good's daughter, Dorca, only four or five years old, were in prison. By the time the hysteria had run its course, 55 people had been forced to admit they were indeed witches. Of those, 19 were hanged for their supposed crimes.

COTTON MATHER'S ROLE

As Boston's leading clergyman, and the author of *Memorable Providences*, it would have been impossible for Mather *not* to play a part

THE CRUCIBLE

The Salem witch trials became the subject of a hit Broadway play in 1953 with the opening of Arthur Miller's classic drama, *The Crucible*. In it, Miller examines the events that led to the trials, drawing on the era's real historical participants, while using his freedom as an artist to change and develop those characters to meet the needs of the play.

But although the play *is* about the Salem witch trials, its real subject is the McCarthyism that was taking place in the United States while *The Crucible* was being written. During that period, America's fear of communism and of having communists in its midst was so great that government hearings were held in an attempt to "root out" those believed to be communists. (The term "McCarthyism" was coined in reference to Senator Joseph McCarthy, a leader in the anti-communism crusade.) In fact, it became known as a "witch hunt," as friends accused friends and family members accused other family members of having communist leanings. Those accused of being communists were blacklisted, meaning that they were unable to find work, and they were shunned by their family and former friends.

Today, *The Crucible* is studied in high schools and universities as a classic of American theater, praised for the brilliance of its writing and for its examination of the effects of false accusations and hysteria on a community.

in the proceedings. Indeed, there are many historians who argue that simply by writing *Memorable Providences*, which described in detail what Mather viewed as the problem of witches in New England, that he, in effect, lit the match that started the hysterical fire that swept through Salem.

A close friend of the majority of the men who were to judge the witches, Mather wrote a letter to one of them, John Richards, explaining his views. There are witches, he wrote, whose crimes are so severe that they deserve to be executed, and others whose crimes demanded that they receive lesser punishment. His main point, though, was that identifying and convicting witches was something that had to be done with extreme caution.

Mather strongly urged Richards and his fellow judges not to rely on so-called spectral evidence in reaching their decisions. Spectral evidence is evidence based on dreams and visions. For example, if a witness dreamed that the spirit of an accused witch appeared to her as a black cat that then proceeded to scratch and bite her, that was spectral evidence. Mather believed such evidence should not be allowed in court because he felt that it was easy for devils to assume the shape and spirit of an innocent person, and such evidence could be a means for the devil to cause the innocent to be tried and executed.

Indeed, when Bridget Bishop became the first "witch" to be convicted and hanged based on spectral evidence (one witness claimed that he awoke one night to see Bishop or her likeness sitting on his stomach), Mather went a step further in his objections. He issued a statement, *The Return of Several Ministers*, which was presented to Governor Phips and his council. In it, Mather and 11 other ministers once again argued that spectral evidence should not be enough to try, let alone convict and execute, anyone accused of witchcraft.

Yet, Mather undercut his plea for justice with the last paragraph of the document. He urged that the government continue on with the trials, saying that,

> Nevertheless, We cannot but humbly Recommend unto the Government, the speedy and vigorous Prosecution of such as have rendered themselves obnoxious, according to the

Direction given in the Laws of God, and the wholesome Statutes of the English Nation, for the Detection of Witchcrafts.

—Kenneth Silverman,
The Life and Times of Cotton Mather

It is known that Mather attended some of the trials himself. There, he heard one accused witch after another testify that they had ridden poles through the sky to attend meetings where up to 500 witches conspired to destroy New England. Mary Lacey was asked why the devil wanted to bring harm to the people of Salem. She replied, as quoted by Kenneth Silverman, that, "the Devil would set up his Kingdom there and we should have happy days."

Why would people falsely testify to something like that? The answer, most likely, is fear. As relatives turned on relatives and friends turned on friends, it was noted that the only people who were being executed were those who didn't confess. Confession, telling the judges what they wanted to hear, regardless of whether it was true or not, seemed the easiest way to save one's life.

To Cotton Mather though, as well as to most observers, the testimony both confirmed the need for trials *and* indicated that what was happening in Salem was different than what had affected the Goodwin children. To them, it was apparent that the invisible world was attempting to destroy Christian Israel. Mather was certain of the plot and is quoted by Silverman as writing that "more than One Twenty have Confessed that they have Signed unto a Book, which the Devil show'd them, and Engaged in his Hellish Design of Bewitching and Ruining our Land."

In a landmark sermon given to his congregation on August 4, Mather spelled out the particulars of the conspiracy against the Puritan paradise. He told them that the outbreak of witchcraft at Salem was just the latest attempt by the devil to reclaim New England, which had been *his* dominion until the Puritans had arrived.

Silverman quotes him as saying, "These Monsters have associated themselves to do no less a thing than, *To Destroy the Kingdom of our Lord Jesus Christ, in these parts of the World.*"

Still though, despite what he saw as overwhelming evidence of a conspiracy against the good Puritans, he was filled with doubts on *how* to determine guilt or innocence. Among those who defend his actions during the hysteria, they point out that Mather did not know anyone who did not believe in witches. Even those of his time who criticized him for inflaming the witchcraft scare did not deny that witches existed.

And, in Mather's defense, it must be said that given the time, and given what he thought he knew to be true, he did what he could to help moderate the results of the trials. Unwilling to accept spectral evidence as sufficient to convict, he did lay out what at the time were rather stringent conditions for finding guilt, as discussed by biographer Babette M. Levy.

> If the person confessed, if other confessed witches implicated him, if two or more reliable witnesses had actually seen him do something or know something that showed supernatural power, if his answers in court showed much confusion, if there were suspicious marks on his body, if he owned puppets, and if, in addition, there was spectral evidence, then the judges might be confident that they were dealing with a witch. If he had sold himself completely to the forces of evil, then he should be put to death.

By the standards of the day, this could be considered moderation.

Yet, there were those who even then criticized the trials as nothing more than mob hysteria. Popular opinion began to turn against the trials, perhaps in part because of cases like that of 80-year-old Giles Corey. Corey, a prosperous farmer, had been accused of being

The elderly Giles Corey was accused of being a witch. Because he refused to enter a plea, he was crushed to death. This engraving depicts Corey in prison.

a witch by Ann Putnam, who claimed that the specter of Corey had visited her and asked her to write in the devil's book. She also claimed that a ghost had appeared before her to tell her that it had been murdered by Corey.

After his arrest, Corey refused to enter a plea of either guilty or not guilty. According to the law at the time, a person who refused to plead could be forced to do so. Corey was led to a pit in the field beside the jail, stripped of his clothing, and laid on the ground in the pit. Boards were placed on top of his chest, and then six men lifted heavy stones and placed them, one by one, on his stomach and chest. After two days, Giles was asked to plead innocent or guilty. He refused, and more and more rocks were piled on top of him. Three days after his ordeal had begun, Corey died, slowly crushed to death by the weight of the boulders.

By September of 1692, with the death of Corey, it seemed to many that things had spun completely out of control. The number of accused, including the wife of Governor Phips, continued to grow. And, with a growing belief that innocent people had been executed, both the public and clergy began to speak out against the trials. Even Increase Mather, stalwart Puritan that he was, spoke out against the evidence used to convict, writing along with 14 other leading ministers that,

> This then I declare and testify, that to take the Life of any one, merely because a *Spectre* or Devil, in a bewitched or possessed Person does accuse them, will bring the Guilt of innocent Blood on the Land.
>
> —Kenneth Silverman,
> *The Life and Times of Cotton Mather*

The only leading minister to refuse to sign the document was Cotton Mather, who was concerned that by focusing on the possibility of innocent "witches" being executed that the trials themselves would come to a halt.

He was correct to be concerned. The last hangings occurred on September 22, 1692, bringing to an end the worst stages of the trials. By May of 1693, the last of the accused were found not guilty of the charge of witchcraft. The ugliness of the Salem witch trials was over, to the vast relief of much of the public. So it was with unfortunate timing that, in October of 1692, Cotton Mather published the work for which he is best known today, a book that defended the now unpopular trials.

6

A Changing New England

I have indeed set myself to countermine the whole
PLOT of the Devil, against *New-England*, in every
branch of it, as far as one of my *darkness* can compre-
hend such a *Work of Darkness*

The book was *The Wonders of the Invisible World:
Observations as Well Historical as Theological, upon
the Nature, the Number, and the Operations of the Devils*. Mather suffered tremendous doubt while writing
the book, and was obviously greatly worried about the
reception that the book would receive, based on the
"Author's Defence," he wrote explaining his motives.

. . . there may be few that love the Writer of this book;
but give me leave to boast so far, there is not one

among all this Body of People, whom this *Mather* would not study to serve as well as to love. With such a *Spirit of Love*, is the Book now before us written: I appeal to all *this World*; and if *this* World will deny me the Right of acknowledging so much, I appeal to the *other*, that it is *not written with an Evil Spirit*.

Wonders of the Invisible World reflects Mather's nervousness because it is a rather shapeless mess—a mixture of sermons, bits from English works, letters, examples of witchcraft, as well as a history of five of the Salem trials. Defending the trials on one hand, defensive on the other, proud of his role in them while at the same time hinting at his discomfort at what occurred, the book became, and still remains what Mather, according to Silverman, called "that reviled book."

Not only was it bad timing for Mather that his book came out just as public opinion had turned against the trials, but appearing in print at the same time was his father's book, *Cases of Conscience*, in which Increase Mather came to a very different conclusion than his son. As biographer Kenneth Silverman pointed out, *Wonders of the Invisible World* explains that devils had broke loose in New England; *Cases of Conscience* explains that innocent people were being killed. It was one of the very few times that father and son so publicly disagreed.

As Cotton Mather indicated in his diary, he did receive some praise for his book. But at the same time, he remained unhappy about the book, its reception, and what it had done to his public image. Torn as always between pride and self-abasement, Mather wrote in his journal that "Upon the severest Examination, and the solemnest Supplication, I still think, that for the main, I have, *written Right*."

His self-confidence was further strengthened when, sometime between September 10 and the end of October 1693, he claimed that he received word from a heavenly visitor. For many months, he had been fully occupied with what he saw as the invisible world, the

OBSERVATIONS

As well *Historical* as *Theological*, upon the NATURE, the NUMBER, and the OPERATIONS of the

DEVILS.

Accompany'd with,

I. Some Accounts of the Grievous Molestations, by DÆ-MONS and WITCHCRAFTS, which have lately annoy'd the Countrey; and the Trials of some eminent *Malefactors* Executed upon occasion thereof: with several Remarkable *Curiosities* therein occurring.

II. Some Counsils, Directing a due Improvement of the terrible things, lately done, by the Unusual & Amazing Range of EVIL SPIRITS, in Our Neighbourhood: & the methods to prevent the *Wrongs* which those *Evil Angels* may intend against all sorts of people among us. especially in Accusations of the Innocent.

III. Some Conjectures upon the great EVENTS, likely to befall, the WORLD in General, and NEW ENGLAND in Particular; as also upon the Advances of the TIME, when we shall see BETTER DAYES.

IV. A short Narrative of a late Outrage committed by a knot of WITCHES in *Swédeland*, very much Resembling, and so far Explaining, *That* under which our parts of *America* have laboured!

V. THE DEVIL DISCOVERED: In a Brief Discourse upon those TEMPTATIONS, which are the more Ordinary *Devises* of the Wicked One.

By **Cotton Mather.**

Boston Printed by *Benj. Harris* for *Sam. Phillips.* 1693.

Mather's book *The Wonders of the Invisible World*, which in part defended the witch trials, was published at a time when public favor turned against the practice. It also came to a very different conclusion from a book his father published at the same time.

unseen workings of the devil and his minions. But he had also been looking for physical signs from God. He had been praying for good angels to make themselves known to him.

This was in and of itself a very non-Puritan thing to do. His church believed that while good angels existed, since the time of Christ they no longer appeared to man and existed only in Heaven. Indeed, Increase Mather, as quoted by Silverman, wrote that "it is an unwarrantable and a very dangerous thing, for men to wish, that they might see, and that they might converse with Angels." To the Puritan mind, it would be all too easy for evil spirits to disguise themselves as good ones, thereby leading the trusting into sin.

Mather, though, was confident enough in his own worthiness to continue to pray for good angels to visit him. There were hints at angelic care: on one occasion, Mather was convinced that it was angels who made him so ill that he was unable to board a ship to preach to troops on an island in Boston Harbor. The troops he would have visited became ill with yellow fever, and Mather was certain that he, too, would have caught yellow fever and died without the "angelic intervention."

This, though, was just the leadup to the main event. One night, after hours of praying and fasting, Mather wrote in his diary that he was visited by an angel, on whose shoulders were wings, who told him that his greatest work was still to come. Mather would write books that would become known both in America and in Europe, books that would serve the church well. After the disastrous reception of *Wonders of the Invisible World*, such a prophecy must have brought Mather much comfort indeed.

BRIDGING THE GAP

In the aftermath of the witch trials, Cotton Mather felt the need to take a deep breath and reassess the religious and political situation in New England. With the selection from Great Britain of a new governor, Irish peer Lord Bellomont, it was becoming increasingly clear that the one-time Puritan nation was being redefined along British lines. With Massachusetts no longer an exclusive Puritan outpost, Mather recognized the need to adapt to new realities.

For the next ten years, Mather made it a personal mission to proclaim that New Englanders were not a special people, but were loyal Englishmen. As such, he insisted that New England Congregationalism was restored to the Church of England, and he sought a new spirit of cooperation with other English Protestant groups, Presbyterians in particular.

In many ways, the Puritan spirit was finally broken by King William's Toleration Act of 1689. The act, by guaranteeing Puritans' right to religious freedom, also left them without a reason to fight *for* their freedom. In effect, it made New England Puritanism unnecessary since it removed the very reason why they had fled Great Britain in the first place. Under the spirit of the act, Mather could no longer consider Episcopalians as the enemy of New England. In Massachusetts and throughout New England, the Puritans were becoming just one Protestant group among many, with a resulting loss of influence and power.

Yet at the same time that Mather was preaching a spirit of unification with other Protestant groups and vowing his loyalty to Great Britain, he was also writing texts and giving sermons lamenting the decline in religious values since the days of the first Puritan settlers. In his 1696 text *Things for a Distress'd People to Think Upon*, he begins by praising the heroic greatness of the first to settle in New England, before bemoaning how far they had declined.

> There seems to be a shameful *Shrink*, in all sorts of men among us, from that *Greatness*, and *Goodness*, which adorned

> our Ancestors: We grow *Little* in our Military Matters, *Little* in our Ecclesiastical Matters; we dwindle away, to *Nothing* . . .
>
> —Kenneth Silverman,
> *The Life and Times of Cotton Mather*

As Silverman points out, at the same time that Mather was preaching the new spirit of religious tolerance, he published more works than ever on the need for reformation. He called for Puritanism to return to an idealized "spiritually minded Puritan community of praying families, children who did not play at the rear of the meetinghouse on Sabbaths, boys and girls who shunned mixed dances, cheerfully obedient servants catechized by caring masters, and sailors who sang psalms instead of bawdy songs."

It was typical Cotton Mather. During the Salem witch trials, Mather urged moderation while at the same time encouraging the trials to proceed at full speed. Now, Mather was urging religious reconciliation while at the same time urging Puritans to become more Puritanical. It seems likely that he was continuously torn in this way—drawn to the new more urbane secular society by his desire for fame and fortune, yet maintaining a spirit of religious conservatism in respect for his father and his father's generation. But by trying to play both sides, Mather often found himself pleasing nobody. He faced continuous charges of hypocrisy, of not truly believing anything he was saying or doing.

MAGNALIA CHRISTI AMERICANA

It was in his latter role as defender of traditional Puritanism that he wrote what is considered to be his most important book, a majestic history of New England entitled *Magnalia Christi Americana* (usually translated into English as *The Ecclesiastical History of New England*).

King William III gives his royal ascent to the toleration act of 1689. This act led to a loss of influence and power for the Puritans.

By 1693, with the passing of the first generation of Puritan Americans, the need for such a book became increasingly apparent, while there were still some alive who could remember the early days. Mather, encouraged by the Cambridge Association of Ministers, began writing the book at the end of 1693. He was hopeful that the book would be published in London as early as 1697. But the manuscript was not shipped to London until June 1770.

The actual publication of the book did not go smoothly. Ship after ship arrived from London with no news or reports of delays and lack of interest in the text. Finally, the book, comprised of 800 pages printed in double columns, divided into seven sections, was published in 1702.

In Book I, "Antiquities," Mather tells the story of the exploration and settlements on the Atlantic coast, as well as of the establishment of the New England colonies: Plymouth, Massachusetts Bay, Connecticut, and New Haven. Book II, "Containing The Lives of the Governors and Names of the Magistrates of New-England," tells the life stories of the colonies' rulers. Book III, "The Lives of Sixty Famous Divines, By Whose Ministry The Churches of New-England Have Been Planted and Continued," is the longest of the seven books and tells the stories of the lives of the first generation of colonial ministers.

Book IV, "An Account of the University of Cambridge in New-England," tells the history of Harvard College, the school created to provide New England with its ministers. Book V, "Acts and Monuments of the Faith and Order in the Churches of New-England," tells in detail the ins and outs of the New England way of worship. Book VI, "A Faithful Record of Many Illustrious, Wonderful Providences," gathers together the incidents, both miraculous and punishing, that had occurred to the people of New England. And finally, Book VII, "The Wars of the Lord," is a history of the invasion of New England churches by such enemies as Native Americans, devils, heretics, and the former Governor Andros.

With the book's opening sentence, "I WRITE the *Wonders* of the CHRISTIAN RELIGION, flying from the Depravations of *Europe* to the *American Strand*," Mather makes his intentions plain. The Puritans had come to America to escape European oppression and, through Christianity, create a place for themselves in the New World. Everything in the book, a stirring mixture of fact, faith, and superstition, comes from that simple statement.

Although the book is riddled with errors (Cotton Mather was not a trained historian), the book is still an invaluable source of information, providing much of what is known about the Plymouth settlement and its leaders, as well as the practices and beliefs of the Puritan settlers. But the reason the book is still read is for

CHILDREN

While the Puritans strongly believed that they had a duty to raise their children properly, they also believed that duty was a two-way street. Children, they thought, had duties toward their parents as well: to obey and respect them, to honor them, and to be a blessing upon them. Mather's essay *The Duties of Children to Their Parents* discusses those obligations at length, as well as the punishments that undutiful children will suffer.

Undutiful Children soon become horrid Creatures; for Unchastity, for Dishonesty, for Lying, and all manner of Abominations: And the Contempt which they cast upon the Advice of their Parents, is one thing that pulls down this Curse of God upon them. They who sin against their Parents, are sometimes by God given up to Sin against all the world beside. Mind the Most Scandalous Instances of Wickedness and Villainy; You'll ordinarily find, they were first Undutiful Children, before they fell into the rest of their atrocious Wickedness. . . .

All the Curse of God upon Undutiful Children hitherto, is but the Death, riding the Pale Horse in the Revelation; whereof 'tis said, Hell followed. I am after to tell you, That the Vengeance of Eternal Fire, will the portion of Undutiful Children after all; Children that cast Contempt upon their Parents, God will cast into the Vengeance of Eternal Fire at the Last, and into Everlasting Contempt.

—Cotton Mather, *The Duties of Children to their Parents*

Source: http://www.spurgeon.org/phil/mather/dut-chi.htm

the opportunity to hear the singular voice of Cotton Mather: learned, witty, wordy (the opening sentence of the life of Governor Phips runs 254 words), and insistent.

The book makes clear Mather's literary ambitions, his dream of writing the great American epic, and in it he achieves something of great and lasting importance. It remains the book that put America on the cultural map, a book whose voice can be heard later in writers as disparate as Herman Melville and Walt Whitman.

It is no wonder that in 1963, when a panel of leading scholars set out to select 1,800 books out of the entire literary output of 350 years of American writing to be in the White House Library, *Magnalia* was one of those chosen. As Babette Levy said, "In fact, Cotton Mather's history or epic, as you will, is the only representative in the library of the thinking and writing of colonial New England."

PERSONAL TRAGEDIES

In the midst of all his hard work—the Salem witch trials, the writing of *Magnalia*, his everyday work as a clergyman—Mather suffered a series of tragedies that would have broken a lesser man.

But then again a lesser man might not have had Mather's faith or his belief that he was favored by providence. He received sign after sign that it was so. On several occasions while traveling, he noted that storms were delayed until he had safely returned home. Once, he wrote in his journal, traveling to Salem and Ipswich, the road was suddenly filled with a "strange Descent of Hundreds of Bears," but he suffered no harm. On another occasion, needing a new cloak, he reminded himself of Christ being stripped of his clothing and told himself that he would never lack for proper clothing. At that very moment, a woman in his congregation presented him with a new and expensive cloak.

Despite this obvious sign of God's love, Mather also received what he saw as signs of God's displeasure, or of God's need to test Mather's faith. By the year 1696, when Mather was 33 years old, he and his wife had had six children, four of whom had already died.

A son, Increase Mather, Jr., was born in 1699, answering one of Mather's prayers by becoming the first of his male children to survive, but the tragedies would only continue.

In May of 1702, Abigail Mather was already ill when she miscarried a son. She didn't recover and was still ill six months later when a smallpox epidemic hit Boston. Eight-year-old Nibby, five-year-old Nancy, and three-year-old Increase all became ill with small pox. The children all recovered, but on December 1, 1702, Abigail died.

Mather was devastated at the loss of his beloved wife. In his journal, he wrote "I had never yet seen such a black Day in all the Time of my pilgrimage. *The Desire of my Eyes* is this day to be taken from me." At her funeral, Mather gave each attendee a copy of one of his works, containing a 12-line poem pasted into the book, quoted by Norma Jean Lutz, that began, "Go then, My DOVE, but now no longer *mine*! Leave *Earth*, and now in *heavenly Glory* shine."

Abigail's death caused Mather, momentarily at least, to question his faith. He felt that he had received reassurances from heaven, moments of prophecy that he called "Particular Faith" that his wife would live. How then, could God have let her die? Perhaps, he told himself, God took his wife to remind Mather that he, too, was mortal. Or, perhaps, God had, in the moment of Particular Faith, only let Mather know that he had heard his prayer. How God would answer the prayer, what God's intentions were, would remain a mystery.

Whatever the reason, he would not remain a widower for long. Just two months after Abigail's death, a young woman, probably named Katharine Maccarty, proposed marriage to him, telling Mather that she found him irresistible. While the 43-year-old Mather found himself attracted to the 23-year-old, his congregation was strongly against the match.

Giving into community pressure and the fear that marriage with her would damage his name, Mather turned to another woman to court. Her name was Elizabeth Hubbard, and her house was conveniently located just two doors down from his. She was a widow of four years, nearly 30 years old, and, quoted by Lutz, in Mather's own words "a Gentlewoman of Piety and Probity, and a most unspotted Reputation; a Gentlewoman of good Witt and Sense, and Discretion at ordering a Household; a Gentlewoman of incomparable Sweetness in her Temper, and Humor; a Gentlewoman honourably descended and related; a very comely person."

The two were married in August of 1703, less than a year after the death of his first wife, Abigail. It would be the start of a new family for him, as well as the beginning of a slow period of decline in Mather's influence and authority.

7

The Most Prominent Minister in America

Increase Mather was now in his sixties, and as was generally the case, in uncertain health. In the words of Kenneth Silverman, "As the new century opened, Cotton Mather was newly remarried, nearing 40, and about to replace his father as the most prominent minister in America."

But as always, Increase exaggerated the seriousness of his condition, once again warning his congregation that his days were numbered. "It is but a very little Time that I have now to be in the World," he told them in 1703, as quoted by Silverman. "*I must shortly put off this my Tabernacle.*" It would be another 20 years, however, before he actually died.

As Increase Mather lessened his connection with the North Church, his son's prominence continued to grow. With a membership of probably around 1,500 people, it remained the largest church in New England. Cotton Mather took his responsibilities to his flock seriously, working to preach, as quoted by Silverman, "as excellent and well studied Sermons as ever I can and contrive all my public Exercises in the most edifying manner that I am able."

Writing a weekly sermon took a great deal of time and effort, usually seven hours worth per sermon. Many factors went into selecting the subject. Sometimes he based it on a dream. Sometimes he received inspiration from a local event such as a thunderstorm or blizzard. Other sermons were geared to a specific public event—an execution, a funeral, or even Election Day. But whatever the subject, the sermons were long by today's standards, generally running from an hour and a half to nearly three hours in length.

Weekly preaching was just a small part of his responsibilities to his flock. He also kept the records for the church, made visits to the homes of his congregants, baptized and catechized children, performed marriages (52 of them in 1709 alone), appeared at funerals, provided letters of recommendation and reference, and worked with private religious societies, up to 20 at any given time.

Many of his pastoral visits were devoted to comforting the sick and dying. Mather himself estimated that by the time he was 34 years old, he had attended the death beds and witnessed the deaths of hundreds, even thousands, of people. His work as a minister never seemed to cease. But no matter what he was doing, he was *always* a minister. His congregation's needs, and his responsibility to serve them as a model, were always his top priority.

But it was in the sheer volume of his writing, in his efforts to use his prominence to reach as wide an audience as possible, that he gained his greatest level of fame and influence. Between 1702 and 1713 he published more than 135 works, and for the rest of his life he averaged 10 published works per year. By the end of his life, he had published 388 separate titles! No other New England minister came close; indeed, it is likely that he published more than all the New England ministers before his time combined.

The subject of his work varied greatly, from shorter works such as funeral sermons on women and an elegy to his beloved schoolmaster Ezekiel Cheever, to his monumental *Magnalia*. Some were written for specific audiences. *Family-Religion, Excited and Assisted* (1705) was sent to 1,000 families throughout New England. *Sailour's Companion* (1709), urging sailors to avoid indulging in dirty language and vice, was to be found on nearly every sailing ship leaving New England.

Indeed, Mather wrote so many titles on so many different subjects aimed at diverse audiences that it seems likely that nearly every family in New England (and many overseas) owned at least one of his publications. It seems not at all unlikely that by 1710 Cotton Mather was the best-known person in America.

And that wasn't all he wrote. Many thousands of pages were written that were never published in his lifetime. Mather also lived in an age of letter-writing and maintained a voluminous correspondence with friends throughout New England and Europe. And while it is unknown just how many letters he wrote, consider this: One single ship bound for England in 1702 was carrying more than 30 of his letters.

But given Mather's continuous self-doubt, it shouldn't be surprising that even his enormous literary output gave him cause for concern. Why, he constantly asked himself, was he writing so much? Was it for the glory of God? Was it to assist his parishioners? Or, was it simply for his own glorification? He wrote in his journal, ". . . that particular Lust, my Pride . . . affections of Grandeur, and Inclinations to be thought Somebody." He even admonished himself for having written too many books for somebody of his "small Attainments."

He wasn't the only one to question his seemingly never-ending flood of literary output. Mather noted in his journal that some people thought less of him for writing so many books. Even his own father, as cited by Silverman, condemned the publishing of too many books as a "Vanity which the Earth Groans under." Increase even wrote in a preface for one of his son's books that perhaps time that should be spent reading the Bible was being spent reading the works of men!

None of the criticism, however, diminished the flow of words coming from Cotton Mather's pen. Instead, he began to take a more defensive position. Some of his works were published anonymously. In others, he would preface the work by saying that "others" had begged him to write it. Mather wrote that of course he would do the person the favor of writing the book, regardless of what others might say.

WANING POLITICAL INFLUENCE

Although Mather remained the dominant minister of his time, his political influence was fading, due to a long-standing feud with the new governor, Joseph Dudley.

The two men had a long and complicated relationship. Both Increase and Cotton Mather had been friends with Dudley and were even related to him through marriage. But when Dudley went to work for the hated Governor Andros as censor of the colony press and as chief justice of the Superior Court, both Mathers turned against him, considering him a traitor to Massachusetts.

When Andros fell from power, so did Dudley, and it seemed to many that his political career had ended. But when acting governor William Stoughton died, Dudley set out to do what he could to gain the appointment and return to New England from London. He sent a series of letters to all of New England's most powerful men, begging for their support. Among those men was Cotton Mather.

Mather and Joseph Dudley clashed over how Dudley managed Queen Anne's War, the second war fought between France and England for control of North America.

Initially, Mather ignored Dudley's letters. Eventually though, after Dudley told Mather that living abroad had changed his attitudes toward New England, his resistance softened. In typical Mather fashion, he wrote a letter that seemed at the same time to both criticize and endorse Dudley. Regardless of the mixed message, Dudley used Mather's seeming endorsement to obtain the position.

It was one of the biggest mistakes of Mather's career. As governor, Dudley proved a disaster. Ignoring Mather's advice to be fairhanded in his appointments, Dudley gave office only to his supporters, a small group composed mainly of Anglicans and overseas

QUEEN ANNE'S WAR

Queen Anne's War was the second in a series of four so-called French and Indian wars fought by France and their Native American allies against England in North America for control of the continent. The fighting took place throughout New England and eastern Canada and started with a series of raids in western New England by the French and Native Americans against English settlements. During a French and Indian raid of Deerfield, Massachusetts, 50 of the town's 300 citizens were killed, and more than 100 were captured, including Cotton Mather's cousin, Eunice. Eunice ultimately decided to remain with her captors and married into the tribe.

The war also involved the British fighting against the Spanish in the South. This is because the war actually began not as a battle over the North American continent, but as part of a

merchants. Within a few years, Dudley, who ignored and alienated the original Puritan settlers, was one of the most hated men in the region. Neither Cotton Mather nor his father approved of Dudley's actions or his decisions. But, it was now clear that the days when the Puritan leaders had any significant influence in political affairs were long over.

The two men disagreed over nearly everything. Mather pretended to support Dudley, in public at least, while criticizing him in private and doing everything he could to have him removed from office. Dudley's handling of Queen Anne's War only added to the pair's mutual distrust. Finally, the break became personal when Dudley appointed John Leverett as president of Harvard, a position that Mather had badly wanted for himself. (Increase Mather had served larger war in Europe to stop a possible unification of the French and Spanish thrones under one monarch, which would have upset the European balance of power. Indeed, it is only in the United States that it is known as Queen Anne's War, reflecting the American colonial practice of naming wars after the reigning monarch. In Canada, Great Britain, and France, this same war is referred to as the North American theater of the War of the Spanish Succession.

In fact, the war finally ended not because of events in North America, but because of the signing of the treaties of Utrecht (1713) and Rastatt (1714) in Europe. As a result of the war, Philip V remained king of Spain but was removed from the French line of succession, ending the possibility of a union of the two kingdoms. In North America, the British won control of Acadia (now known as Nova Scotia), the island of Newfoundland, and the Hudson Bay region, as well as the Caribbean island of St. Kitts.

as Harvard's president from 1692 to 1701, and Cotton wanted to continue the family's influence there.)

What had once been private became public, as both sides declared war against each other. Mather spoke out and wrote publicly against the governor, reminding him that it had been Mather's influence that had helped gain him the position of governor in the first place. In response, Dudley intercepted Mather's correspondence and made it public, abused and mocked him publicly, and even published a pamphlet reminding the public about Mather's short-lived relationship with Katherine Maccarty.

In addition, encouraged by Dudley's attacks on Mather, others now felt free to attack him as well. The times were indeed changing in Massachusetts Bay; the absolute control that the first and second generation of Puritans had held over all aspects of life in the colony was quickly ending. Kenneth Silverman gives this as an example: In 1688, it was "devils" who wanted Martha Goodwin to celebrate Christmas in a jovial manner. By 1711, boys and girls in the North Church were openly celebrating Christmas as a holiday, with feasts, parties, and dances.

From being an object of respect, Mather began to become an object of derision, a symbol of times already past. People were now brave enough to mock him; young men would meet outside of his window at night to sing "profane and filthy songs." Overseas, a group of London Quakers published a broadside attacking Mather. And, in the historian John Oldmixon's two-volume *The British Empire in America*, he attacked *Magnalia Christi Americana* as being nothing more than a schoolboy's exercise, describing it as,

> So confus'd in the Form, so trivial in the Matter, and so faulty in the Expression, so cramm'd with Puns, Anagrams, Acrosticks, Miracles and Prodigies, that it rather resembles School Boys Exercises Forty Years ago, and *Romish* Legends, than the Collections of an Historian bred up in a Protestant Academy . . . [*Magnalia*] is a sufficient Proof, that Man may have read hundreds of Latin Authors, and be qualify'd to construe them, may have spent his Youth in a College, and be bred up in Letters, yet have neither Judgment to know how to make a Discourse perspicuous, nor Eloquence to express his Sentiments so that they may please and persuade . . .
>
> —Kenneth Silverman,
> *The Life and Times of Cotton Mather*

For the remainder of his life, Mather felt the pain caused by those criticisms.

He still had his fair share of admirers, however. In May 1710, the University of Glasgow awarded him with a Doctor of Divinity degree, the highest scholastic honor then available. Mather was the school's first American recipient. But although he was pleased to receive it, once again, he felt a large amount of guilt for the pride he felt in the honor. He even questioned whether or not he should wear the ring he received as a token of his honorary doctorate.

Back home in Boston, even this high honor earned Mather criticism. A gentleman named John Banister published a poem, quoted by Kenneth Silverman, regarding Mather's "Diploma," describing him not as a distinguished citizen of Boston but a wordy egomaniac.

> *On C. Mr's Diploma*
> The mad enthusiast, thirsting after fame,
> By endless volum'ns thought to raise a name.
> With undigested trash he throngs the Press;
> Thus striving to be great, he's the less.

To Mather, who constantly questioned the motives behind his "striving to be great," no criticism could have hurt more.

BONIFACIUS

Facing what he saw as a never-ending series of malicious and unwarranted attacks, Mather decided his best strategy was to turn the other cheek. He would respond not with criticism of his own, but with a new determination to spend his life "Doing Good."

For example, Tuesday mornings were spent contemplating those he saw as his personal enemies and considering, as quoted by Silverman, *"what good may I do unto them?"* He became determined to replace evil with good, so whenever he found himself thinking ill of someone he would "extinguish it, and contradict it, with forming a good Thought, that shall be directly contrary to it." Indeed, Mather began to see the privilege of doing good as a reward from God to well-meaning men (such as himself) who found themselves angered by the actions or words of others.

Doing good became such a focus of his life that he even changed the way he wrote in his diary, making the focus of each day's entry the act of good that he had performed that particular day. In one five-day period in February of 1711, he noted that he and his family spent an evening reading from an appropriate Book of Piety. The next day he had his nephew come visit him and gave him a copy of the *Religion of the Morning*. The next day he sent religious tracts to a boat leaving for Scotland. The next day he helped to recruit members for the Society for the Suppression of Disorders. And on the final day he helped to obtain clothing for an elderly man in need. As he wrote in his journal in 1713, "The grand Intention of my Life is *To Do Good*."

He wanted others to "do good" as well and published a major piece entitled *Bonifacius: An Essay Upon the Good That Is to Be Devised and Designed* on that very subject. In it, as quoted by Silverman, he offered "humble proposals of unexceptional methods" to business persons, ministers, merchants, school masters, magistrates, and physicians in ways to do good. He advised them to help the poor and misfortunate, suggested that the wealthy should provide scholarships for orphans, and urged lawyers to provide *pro bono*, or free, legal work for the poor and needy.

Bonifacius proved to be an enormous success, going through numerous reprintings and influencing countless Americans. Benjamin Franklin, although just four years old when the book was first published, was heavily influenced by it, as he wrote years later, saying that it produced,

. . . such a turn of thinking, as to have an influence on my conduct for life; for I have always set a greater value on the

character of a *doer of good*, than on any other kind of reputation; and if I have been . . . a useful citizen, the Public owes
the advantage of it to that book.

—Kenneth Silverman,
The Life and Times of Cotton Mather

It is interesting to note that even in *Bonifacius*, Mather could not
help but display the anger and resentment that helped fuel his desire
to do good. He wrote, "There is not any revenge more heroic, than
that which torments envy by doing good." In other words, Mather
saw doing good not just as a good unto itself, but as a way of aveng-
ing oneself against those who do you wrong.

Some of his ways of doing good seem inappropriate to modern
eyes, however. For example, seeing unconverted Native Americans as
children of the devil, he spoke of
the need to redeem them through
conversion to Christianity. He
felt the same way about blacks
being held as slaves throughout
New England (Mather owned
slaves himself). Although he saw
nothing wrong with slavery, he
urged that blacks, too, as cited by
Silverman, should be "christian-
ized," telling slave owners that
"they are *Men*, and not *Beasts*
that you have bought."

But although such attitudes
strike us as painfully wrong,
Mather was, in many ways, a man
of his time, with the attitudes and
beliefs of those surrounding him.

Founding Father Benjamin
Franklin was influenced by
Mather's *Bonifacius*.

On the other hand, in some ways, as evidenced by his continuing interest in science, he was more advanced than many around him. To Cotton Mather, serving the interests of science, helping to advance human knowledge, was not only worthy of itself, but just one more way of doing good.

He began a long correspondence with the Royal Society in London, describing the New World to British scientists, in what he called "Curiosa Americana." These included examples of fossils, plant and animal life, scientific oddities such as a black snake that was said to have fallen from the sky, cures appearing in dreams, and "tiny wounds that have proved mortal and extremely grievous wounds that have not"—all the things that Mather thought were to be found only in America.

Mather's communications with the Royal Society was one instance when his attempts to do good were rewarded. Richard Waller, secretary of the Royal Society, wrote back to Mather in July 1713, informing him, as quoted by Silverman, that his first series of Curiosa "very well pleased and Entertained" the members. Silverman notes that Mather wrote back, hinting that he'd very much appreciate becoming a member of the society itself, while, in typical fashion, denying that he was at all worthy of the honor. "I cannot presume so much upon my own merits as to dream of being thought worthy to be admitted a member of that more than illustrious Society."

The hint worked. In October of 1713, Cotton Mather received word that he would indeed be made a fellow of the Royal Society. From that time on, he often printed the designation "F.R.S." (Fellow of the Royal Society) on the title pages of his books, along with his "D.D." from Glasgow. Mather was not only justifiably proud of his achievement—he was only the eighth colonist selected to one of the most prestigious scientific bodies in the world—but saw it as a sign that God wanted to encourage him to continue in his efforts to do good.

It would, however, be one of the last encouraging signs he would be receiving from God for quite some time. Mather's life, which had already seen more than its share of tragedy, was soon to see even more.

8

Family Troubles

Despite all of his fame and the awards and recognition he received, it never seemed to be enough. Mather, especially as he grew older, began more and more to display the anger and wrath that have become the traits that he is known for today.

Hurt by the disrespect he felt he had been shown by men such as Dudley, he began to lash out more and more angrily against those he felt were against him. He seemed to become two different people, one who was able to write in his journal or to the Royal Society about the power of logic and reason one moment, while attacking those he saw as his enemies in his sermons in the next, saying that,

[The minister] is above the reach of Hurt from your Malignity. You do but add unto his *Crown*, as often as you Express your Disaffection to him. Do, Go on to make him the Object of your Venom; Throw all the Dirt of a *Street* upon him, if you please . . . You will *Wound* your selves, and none but your selves, Wretches . . .

Silly Children, the Minister of God is above all your Silly Attempts. You can't hurt *him*. If the Wrath of God, had not left you bereft of your Wits, you would feel, that you hurt but *your selves*. Your venomous *Arrows* are all Shot against a Rock.

> —Kenneth Silverman,
> *The Life and Times of Cotton Mather*

Astonishingly, he could also praise others for their kindness to poor children, while lashing out at those very children in a sermon, promising them an eternity in Hell.

There are *Children*, whose Doom will be to be *Burnt to Death*, In the *Day of the Lord that shall burn like an Oven*. There are *Children*, whom God will send into *Everlasting Fire with the Devil and his Angels*. And what *Children*? *Wicked* Children; The *Children* that makes themselves the *Children of the Devil* . . .

> —Kenneth Silverman,
> *The Life and Times of Cotton Mather*

It seems likely that, given the events to come, he grew to regret such sermons.

DEATH AND MORE DEATH

Now in his middle age, Mather was the head of a larger family than any he'd had previously. There were the four children that had

MUSIC

There is one aspect of Cotton Mather's influence on American life and culture that has received little notice, and that is his impact on American music and music education. Like many Puritans, Mather valued psalmody, or the singing of psalms or hymns, largely because he considered it to be a form of prayer. Of course, Mather also had a special appreciation for singing, due to his use of song to help control his stammer. At any rate, Mather encouraged his congregation to sing as an act of daily devotion, and he regularly sang with his family as part of their daily prayers, as well as by himself during his frequent fasts and prayer vigils. He also composed a large number of hymns, some of which were collected in a book, *Songs of the Redeemed* (1697), of which no copy is known to have survived.

Not only did Mather encourage singing in religious services, but he also argued that singers should be taught to read music in order to improve the quality of singing. This, in turn, started

survived of the nine he'd had with his first wife: Katherine, Abigail ("Nibby"), Hannah ("Nancy"), and Increase Jr. And by 1711, he and second wife Elizabeth had had four children: Elizabeth (1704), Samuel (1706), Nathanael (1709), and Jerusha (1711). Nathanael survived only to the age of six months, but at the age of nearly 50, Mather was now the father of five daughters and two sons ranging in age from newborn to 22.

By all accounts, despite the anger and disappointment that Mather often displayed toward the outside world, he was a good and loving father. As a Puritan, it was incumbent upon him to raise his children well, without harshness, to instill in them an understanding of their parents' love for them. He spent much time with them (he a long-running argument throughout early America. While city dwellers accepted Mather's ideas, those in the more rural, conservative areas fought against the idea of a formalized role for music in church, attacking it as "Catholic" and decidedly non-Puritanical.

In the long run, Cotton Mather won the debate. And, by urging the development of musical literacy in New England, he played an important early role in the development of the arts in America. In 1721, his nephew Thomas Walter published *The Grounds and Rules of Musick Explained*, one of the first two books published in America on music instruction. Within 50 years of its publication, New England saw the creation of singing schools, which led to the need for singing masters to lead them, which ultimately led to the need for American composers to write for them. In 1770, the first volume of American-composed music, *The New-England Psalm Singer*, was published. Its composer, William Billings, was a direct beneficiary of Mather's encouragement of America's musical education.

was generally home when not preaching or making pastoral visits), and he often called the children into his study to speak to them or to pray.

Indeed, the entire family met every morning at nine o'clock (and again in the evening) for religious education, prayer, Bible reading, and psalm singing. The children who were in school would come home to take part in the worship meetings. They were also required to keep a daily journal, in which they would write down their thoughts about religious matters. In addition, he provided each child with a one-shelf library taken from his own books, giving them new books to read each week. And of course, his children were always in his prayers; they were the most important thing in his life.

This makes all the more tragic the events of early winter 1713, which saw the worst epidemic of measles in the history of colonial America. Within two weeks Mather's entire family was struck with the disease, including his wife, Elizabeth, who had just given birth to a set of twins, Martha and Elezaor. "Help Lord," Mather wrote in his journal, "and look mercifully on my poor, sad, sinful Family . . ."

Always looking for ways to do good, Mather's concern about the epidemic went well beyond his immediate family. He issued a pamphlet, *Letter About a Good Management under the Distemper of the Measles,* which has been called by one historian of medicine, cited by Norma Jean Lutz, "one of the very few classics of early American medicine."

Drawing on his knowledge and interest in science, Mather, as quoted by Kenneth Silverman, matter-of-factly described the stages of the disease and urged against overtreatment, which could only worsen the disease. "*Don't kill 'em!* That is to say, With mischievous Kindness. Indeed, if we stop there, and said no more, this were enough to save more *Lives,* than our *Wars* have destroyed."

Unfortunately, his good advice to let the disease simply run its course wasn't enough to stop the deaths in his own family. His wife, Elizabeth, was the first to die. The infant children went next, along with a long-time servant. The last to die was his "dear little Jerusha." In some ways, the possibility that his youngest surviving daughter would be taken from him was the hardest for him to accept. He wrote in his journal that, "I begg'd, I begg'd, that such a bitter Cup, as the Death of that lovely child, might pass from me."

Jerusha died on November 22, 1713. "My lovely Jerusha expires . . . Lord, I am oppressed; undertake for me." The pain that Mather felt at the loss of so many members of his family was nearly unbearable. But he used his pain in his sermons to his congregation, presenting himself as an example of one who had, as quoted by Silverman, "the Happiness to do the more Good for every Evil that befalls me."

A BRIEF RULE

To guide the Common-People of

NEW-ENGLAND

How to order themselves and theirs in the

Small Pocks, or Measels.

A Brief Rule was a printed guide to the treatment of measles in New England in 1677. Measles struck Mather's family in 1713.

Mather was certain that God gave him the strength to survive his losses so that he could acknowledge that love by accepting the will of God.

It was apparent to Mather that God was asking him to sacrifice much and that he would, in time, be rewarded for his sacrifice. Yet, at the same time, in a moment of utter humanness, he wrote on the back cover of one of his journals the names of all the fifteen children that he had fathered. Next to the list, he wrote down these horrible numbers, quoted by Kenneth Silverman.

Of 15,
Dead, 9
Living, 6

Mather had had two successful marriages, and after a period of suitable mourning, it would be time for Cotton Mather to once again find himself a new wife. The third marriage, however, would not by any reckoning be considered a success.

LYDIA LEE GEORGE

Lydia Lee George, the daughter of the esteemed Rev. Samuel Lee, was a woman with a family heritage of intellectual distinction and wealth. She had one additional thing in her favor: A recent widow, George had inherited a great estate, including servants and household goods, as well as stocks and profits from a wide array of business interests.

At first, George had no interest in Mather or even in remarrying at all. Their first meeting, on March 21, 1715, did not go well. Mather was not willing to take no for an answer though, and he persisted in his courtship, despite her often dismissive attitude toward him. It seemed, in fact, that her slightly contemptuous attitude toward him only deepened his feelings toward her, for his journals indicate that the depth of his romantic feelings for her far exceeded those he had for his first two wives.

He finally wore down her resistance, and on June 24 the couple signed a prenuptial agreement. While many people would assume that "prenups" are a modern invention, many of the colonies allowed such agreements, which allowed women to protect their property rights after marriage. Under the terms of the agreement signed by Mather and George, her property and estate would remain her own. Ten days later, on July 5, 1715, the couple married.

Mather was pleased with his new marriage, and even the death of his daughter Katharine in December 1716, did not change that. Instead, he consoled himself over his loss with the publication of *Victorina* (1717), a sermon on the satisfaction that one received from true piety, which included an account of his beloved daughter's life.

Along with the happiness of his new marriage, came an improved relationship with the colonial government. A new governor, Samuel Shute, had arrived in Boston in October 1716, and Mather was, as quoted by Silverman, determined to "improve my Acquaintance, which I am like to have with him, for all the good Purposes imaginable." His efforts to befriend the new governor paid off, and he had the best relationship with him that he'd had with any governor since Phips.

The new feelings of harmony that Mather was feeling in his marriage and in his relationship with the new government spread to his religious life as well. As we have seen, for many years he had attempted to bring together Congregationalists and Presbyterians to unify the two main Protestant churches. His previous efforts had failed, but, as we have also seen, Mather was not a man to give up easily.

In his *The Stone Cut out of the Mountain* (1716), he listed 14 maxims on which all Christians (with the exception of

Catholics) could agree. Within the next year, he reduced that number to three: a belief in the Trinity, the recognition that only Christ could bring salvation, and the need to love one's neighbor as an expression of love for Christ. This new "universal religion" was light years away from his early expression of belief in angels and witches, and it makes the latter-period Mather a symbol of religious tolerance, far removed from his fiery past.

A TROUBLED SON

This brief period of harmony and good feelings was soon to come to an end, as personal and financial problems threatened his newfound happiness.

His son Increase Jr., known as "Cresy," was proving to be the proverbial problem child. Both Cotton and his father tried to talk to and pray for the younger Increase, hoping to lead him away from a life of "sin" and toward a life of useful piety. "My miserable, miserable, Son Increase!" Cotton wrote in his journal. "The wretch has brought himself under public Trouble and Infamy by bearing in a Night-Riot, with some detestable Rakes in the town."

Their relationship fell into a predictable pattern: Cresy would disappoint his father and Cotton would decide to give up on him, but then he'd forgive Cresy once again and the pattern would repeat itself. For his part, Cotton Mather could not conceive why and how he could have fathered such a troubled child, and he worried that Creasy would never find salvation. "Suppose," he is quoted by Silverman as having asked himself, "that a Child of my singular Love and Hope, should fall into Sin, and be after wondrous Means of Recovery, yet so abandoned by God, and so ensnared in Vice, that there may [be] terrible Cause to fear lest he prove a Cast-away?"

To make matters worse, Cotton's marriage to Lydia Lee George quickly descended into his own personal nightmare. He wrote in a private notebook he kept apart from his regular journal, as quoted by Silverman, that "The Consort, in whom I flattered myself with the View and Hopes of an uncommon Enjoyment, has dismally confirmed it to me, that our *Idols* must prove our *Sorrows.*"

It appears that George was not mentally stable and suffered from periods of deep depression followed with fits of wild uncontrollable anger. Today, of course, such an illness could be understood and treated. But in those days prior to psychologists, therapists, and medications, there was nothing that Mather (or George) could do but suffer. In his journal he called 1718, the first year of her attacks, "a Year of such Distresses with me, as I have never seen in my Life before."

And things got even worse. Although Mather was no businessman, in 1716 he agreed to manage the financial interests of the estate of Nathan Howell, who had been married to Lydia's daughter by her previous marriage. It proved to be a mistake of epic proportions. The estate was in complete disarray, there were complications everywhere Mather looked, and by early 1719, he found himself being brought into court on a regular basis to answer claims against the estate.

The man who had considered himself a respectable model citizen, who took pride in himself and his standing in the community, now regularly found himself on the wrong side of the law. It was a profoundly humiliating experience. A friend, quoted by Silverman, wrote that Mather lived in state of constant dread: "Every one that knocks at his door surprises him, that his heart dies within him, as he sayes, fearing there is an Arrest to be serv'd on him, or some body to dun him for a Debt."

Unbelievably, his woes increased even further when problems arose with Governor Shute's administration. Because of Mather's strong support for Shute, the governor's enemies soon became his. It must have seemed to Mather that things had become hopeless, that he was being defeated on all sides. Little did he know, though, that

Boston would soon experience a catastrophe that would become for him a moment of personal vindication. He wrote about the beginnings of the event in his journal on May 26, 1721.

> The grievous Calamity of the *Small-Pox* has now entered the Town. The Practice of conveying and suffering the *Small-Pox* by *Inoculation*, has never been used in *America*, nor indeed in our Nation. But how many Lives might be saved by it, if it were practiced?

9

A Return to Science

In April 1721, the *Seahorse*, a ship from Tortugas in the West Indies, brought to Boston a new outbreak of smallpox, a disease that seemed to strike the city at alarmingly regular intervals. By the end of May, the disease had reached epidemic proportions, and fear of the disease drove hundreds to flee the city. Businesses shut down, and funeral bells were heard tolling at all hours of the day and night.

For those of us living in the twenty-first century, for whom smallpox is nothing more than a distant memory (it was eradicated in 1979, the first human infectious disease to be eliminated as a risk to mankind), it's difficult to imagine the terror it struck in those living in dread of the disease. Dr. Zabdiel Boylston, a friend of Cotton Mather, described some of the disease's more disturbing effects.

Purple Spots, the bloody and parchment Pox, Hemorahages of Blood at the Mouth, Nose, Fundament, and Privities; Ravings and Deliriums; Convulsions, and other Fits; violent inflammations and Swellings in the Eyes and Throat; so that they cannot see, or scarcely breathe, or swallow anything, to keep them from starving. Some looking as black as the Stock, others as white as a Sheet; in some, the Pock runs into Blisters, and the Skin stripping off, leaves the Flesh raw . . . Some have fill'd with loathsome Ulcers; others have had deep, and fistulous Ulcers in their Bodies, or in their Limbs or Joints, with Rottenness of the Ligaments and Bones: Some who live are Cripples, others Idiots, and many blind all their Days . . .

—Kenneth Silverman,
The Life and Times of Cotton Mather

Of those who contracted the disease, between 20 and 60 percent died; among children, nearly 80 percent died.

During the worst days of his stutter, Mather had given serious thought to becoming a physician. Although he gave up the idea of making it a career, his interest in medicine (and the other sciences) never ended. And of course, given his own tragic history of loss through disease, his interest had grown more intense and much more personal. Through his correspondence with the Royal Society, he had learned of a new way to help prevent the disease, a "Wonderful Practice" he hoped, would help stop the epidemic before it became even worse.

On June 7, 1721, Mather wrote a letter to Boston's leading physicians urging that those Bostonians who had not already been stricken by the disease be inoculated. Mather had a rough understanding that smallpox was caused by germs and that millions of germs were to be found in the pustules, the pus-filled blisters that covered the body of those who were sick with the disease. By

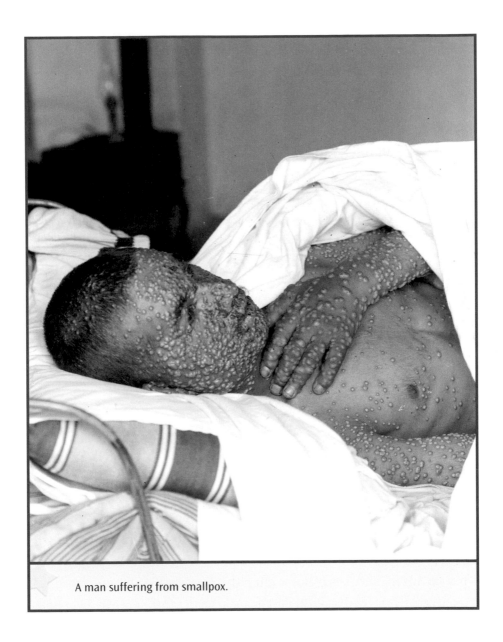

A man suffering from smallpox.

opening up one of those blisters, and then placing the pus into a small cut on someone who was not sick, that person would get a mild case of smallpox that lasted around three days. After that, the patient was immune for life.

He did not get the reaction he expected. Instead of gratitude, the physicians turned on him, attacking him publicly and accusing him of working to perpetuate the disease. This "folk custom" as they called inoculation, had been used for centuries in Africa, India, and China, by godless heathens. The very idea of using the same treatment as atheists scared and angered the population of Boston.

The sole exception to the medical establishment's dismissal of Mather's idea was a young doctor named Zabdiel Boylston. He joined forces with Mather, and bravely standing up against public opinion, Boylston inoculated his six-year-old son, Thomas, against the disease. Thomas developed a mild case of the disease and quickly recovered. Mather's proposal had worked.

Despite the procedure's success, the news of Boylston's experiments and Mather's encouragement of them further alarmed most Bostonians. Mather and Boylston soon found themselves the objects of abuse. "They rave, they rail, they blaspheme, they talk not only like Idiots, but also like Fanaticks, and not only with the physician who began the Experiment, but I also am the object of their fury," Mather noted, as quoted by Lutz.

Boylston was called three times before the city's magistrates and told to stop his work, but three times he refused. Mather continued to support his friend, but despite his concern for the general populace, his deepest concern was for his own family. Two of his children had been born after the last epidemic and were not immune to the disease: Elizabeth, nearly 17, and Sammy, nearly 15. Elizabeth turned to prayer in the hope of staying healthy, but Samuel, who was already attending college, begged his father to allow him to be inoculated.

Given the mood of the town, Mather had his doubts about having his son inoculated, fearing further attacks and worrying that, according to Silverman, the "cursed Clamour of a People strangely and fiercely possessed of the Devil, will probably prevent my saving the Lives of my two Children, from the Small-pox in the Way of Transplantation."

He found himself torn between the two sides: If he didn't give his son the inoculation and he later got the disease and died, Mather would never be able to forgive himself. If he gave it to his son and the inoculation didn't work (a small percentage of those inoculated did die from the inoculation itself), his position in the town would be impossible.

At the advice of his father, Increase, Mather allowed the inoculation to take place, but in secret. "I could not answer it unto God, if I neglected it." A few days after receiving his inoculation, Sammy's fever had risen dangerously high. Mather turned to prayer and decided to open his Bible to a random page, hoping that it would provide him a suitable subject for meditation. The first line he read was this: Go the Way, thy Son liveth.

Even so, Sammy's fever continued to rise until, in what seemed to be a delirium, Sammy requested that he be bled, a standard treatment for many illnesses at that time. A vein was opened, and, surprisingly, he quickly recovered. (Tragically, one month later, Mather's daughter Abigail gave birth to a daughter named Resigned, who died hours before being baptized. Abigail died four days later, the eleventh of Mather's fifteen children to die.)

Despite everything, Mather and Boylston continued their impassioned campaign for inoculation. Most people, though, refused to listen to scientific reason, and on November 14, someone tried to kill Cotton Mather. At around three o'clock in the morning, a "fired Granado" was thrown into his house. Fortunately for all involved, the bomb failed to go off. When it was examined later, a message was found tied to it with a piece of string and cited by Kenneth Silverman as saying, "COTTON MATHER, *You Dog. Dam you, I'll inoculate you with this, with a Pox to you.*"

The failed assassination did nothing to stop the attacks on Mather and his character. Kenneth Silverman notes that he was attacked for his "innate Itch of Writing," for his membership in the Royal Society, and for urging Boylston to proceed with the inoculations without receiving the permission of Boston's medical community first.

Mather felt defeated by the continuous criticism, writing in his journal that by his attempts to do good he had "entirely ruined myself as to this World, and rendered it really too hot a Place for me to continue in." He eventually reached the point, according to Silverman, where he announced to the world that he was going to withdraw from public affairs all together: "*I have done! I have done! I have done* treating you with any more of my Proposals."

By the time the epidemic had run its course in February of 1722, 5,889 Bostonians had become infected, and 844 of them had died. On the other hand, of the 242 patients inoculated by Dr. Boylston, only 6 died. It seems ironic that on one of the few occasions that Mather seemed to be trying to do good without any ulterior motive, he received the most vicious attacks of his career. Indeed, in his journal, Mather made careful note of the fact that if only people had listened to him, many lives would have been saved. It was, in truth, one of the most heroic efforts of his life.

LAST YEARS

Cotton Mather's last years were difficult ones. His father, now 85 years old and in increasingly poor health, made his final appearance at the pulpit of the North Church in September of 1722. His next year was spent in a slow decline, as his aging body finally began to give in to the ravages of time. He was in pain for months, his son usually at his side. Not surprisingly, his last days on earth began with one last premonition. Increase, as quoted by Silverman, told Cotton that "It is now Revealed from Heaven to me, That I shall Quickly, quickly, quickly be fetch'd away to Heaven, and that I shall Die in the Arms of my Son." Three days later, Increase Mather did, in fact, die in his son's arms.

The funeral was one of the largest that Boston had ever seen. "A greater *Funeral*," Cotton wrote in his journal, "than had ever been seen for any *Divine*, in *these* (and some Travellers at it, said, *in any other*) parts of the World." In Increase Mather's will, he gave his black servant, Spaniard, his freedom, and to his son Cotton he left what little he had: his watch, a pendulum clock, a silver tankard, a cloak, his manuscripts, and half of his library. (The other half of his library was divided between his other son, Samuel, who was a preacher in London, and his grandson Mather Byles, the son of his daughter Elizabeth.)

At this time, Cotton Mather assumed his father's position as senior pastor of North Church, and a younger man, the Reverend Joshua Gee, came on as the new associate and Mather's probable successor. Nearing the age of 60, Mather continued his busy schedule of preaching, visiting the sick and needy, and extensively reading and writing, but with the absence of his father, it would never be the same.

This was also the period when his financial situation, brought about by the constant lawsuits arising from the management of the Howell estate, was coming to a head. Mather feared that he was destined to end his days penniless and in prison, and in his journal he bewailed his fate. Indeed, it must have seemed to him that God himself had turned against him. (Others said the same thing as well. Throughout his career, Mather had preached that affliction was God's punishment for sin. Now, people saw *him* as the most afflicted minister in New England, which meant that he must be the greatest sinner!)

It was almost too much for him to bear. Fortunately for him, four members of his congregation, who had heard of his plight, came to him and promised that they would pay off all monies owed. Although he was relieved (he had been reduced to accepting gifts of charity just to support his family), it did not mean that his period of woe was over.

Problems with his wife, Lydia, continued. Her periods of manic anger became more and more frequent. She would have wild displays of temper, pack her bags and leave, then return days or weeks later, loving and apologetic, before the cycle began again. Mather was in despair over what to do about it and found himself powerless to help.

His personal anguish deepened. His father had died. His wife was suffering from severe emotional illness. He had once again been denied the presidency of Harvard that he felt he deserved. But all paled in comparison to the news he received on August 20, 1724. On that date he heard the news that his son Increase, who despite everything had remained his favorite, had drowned when a ship he had been aboard had sunk. "My son *Increase*, is lost, is dead is gone," he wrote in his journal. "Ah! My Son *Increase*! My Son! My Son! My Head is Waters, and my Eyes are a Fountain of Tears! I am overwhelmed!"

He was the twelfth of Mather's children to die. Mourning his son's death, Mather was determined to use it as way to continue his service to God. In that way, his son, who had sinned so much in life, could be seen to have done some good in death. Mather published a series of sermons entitled *The Words of Understanding* (1724), which showed that the anger, disappointment, and resentment he felt throughout his life didn't fade in his old age. In one section, he summed up his life's lesson: man is born to suffer, and that suffering has no end.

> When we are wading thro' some grievous and some tedious Trouble, we are prone to flatter our selves, *Well, this is the last! If I were once got well out of this Trouble, all would be well.* 'Tis a great mistake. There will soon come *another* trouble in the room of that which is gone. Men are *Fools*, if they think, their *mirth* can last any longer, than *Sparks*, or than the *Crackling of thorns under a Pot* . . .
>
> —Kenneth Silverman,
> *The Life and Times of Cotton Mather*

To Mather, those words felt particularly true on August 7, 1726, when his 22-year-old daughter Elizabeth died. Thankfully, it would be the last time he would be obligated to preach a sermon regarding the death of one his children. His health began to fail him, but his interest in the world around him never did.

And the world still remained interested in him. It was in 1727 that he sat for a portrait done by Peter Pelham. The portrait was later sold as a print, the first mezzotint made in the American colonies. And, it seems likely that Mather's portrait was the first ever done of an American that others wanted enough to purchase and hang in their own homes.

Cotton Mather sat for this portrait by artist Peter Pelham in 1727.

THE ANGEL OF BETHESDA

It may not be altogether surprising, given his ongoing interest in science, that in 1724, Cotton Mather wrote what many consider to be the most important American medical book of the colonial period: *The Angel of Bethesda*.

The book was written for the average person, to be used as a medical guide to diagnose and treat illnesses, as well as to suggest rules for preserving one's health. The book covered diseases and ailments ranging from smallpox to foot odor, quoting from more than 250 of the age's medical writers. And while some of his remedies, such as using citrus juice to treat and prevent scurvy, make sense today, others, such as wearing a girdle made of wolf-skin for epilepsy, sticking a needle into a centipede for treating a toothache, using cow's urine as a treatment for asthma, or using the urine of a young boy as a gargle for sore throats, seem antiquated if not outright dangerous.

Mather was unable to publish the book during his lifetime, as he was unable to find a publisher willing to take the financial risk to print the 322-page book. It was finally published in the twentieth century, allowing readers to read and enjoy Mather's curious blend of science, folk medicine, and superstitions.

By the end of 1727, it was apparent that Mather was facing his own death. For him though, as for all Puritans, death was not seen as something to be feared. It was something to be welcomed. Death would release him from all the pain and grief of daily life and unite him with God. Three days before his death, he was visited by his successor, Joshua Gee, who, according to Kenneth Silverman, recorded his last words. "And is this dying! This all! Is this what I feared when

I prayed against a hard death! It is no more than this! O I can bear this! I can bear it! I can bear it!"

Cotton Mather died on the day after his sixty-fifth birthday, February 13, 1728. He was a man who had outlived his time—a relic of a time of Puritan certainty, of witch trials, and religious intolerance. To us today, that is the image that remains: that of a bigoted man, intolerant of dissent; a man both superstitious and of absolute moral certainty.

Yet, at his funeral, even those who had attacked him during his final years came to mourn him. They remembered his untiring devotion to his congregation, his learning, his wit, his extraordinary written output, and how his faith had enabled him to continue to live his life fully, no matter what tragedies befell him.

They eulogized him as the first colonist who had reached out to Old Europe through his correspondence and writings. They praised him as the first man to write at length about the New World without ever having been to the Old World; the man who helped introduce America to the rest of the world. He was remembered as one of the towering figures of his time.

Chronology

1663	Cotton Mather is born in Boston, Massachusetts.
1664	Cotton's father, Increase, is ordained as minister and teacher of the Second (North) Church in Boston.
1675	Cotton Mather enters Harvard at the age of 12, one of the youngest students ever admitted. Struggles to overcome his stutter.

TIMELINE

1689 Publishes his account of the Goodwin family and witchcraft in New England, *Memorable Providences, Relating to Witchcrafts and Possessions*

1675 Enters Harvard at the age of 12

1663

1689

1663 Cotton Mather is born in Boston, Massachusetts

1686 Marries Abigail Phillips

1680	Enters the ministry and preaches his first sermon, in the church of his grandfather Richard Mather.
1685	Overcoming his father's objections, becomes an associate with his father at North Church.
1686	Marries Abigail Phillips.
1688	Becomes involved with the Goodwin family, whose children are said to have fallen under the spell of witches.
1689	Publishes his account of the Goodwin family and witchcraft in New England, *Memorable Providences, Relating to Witchcrafts and Possessions*.
1692	Outbreak of the witch trials in Salem Village. Despite Mather's objections to the use of

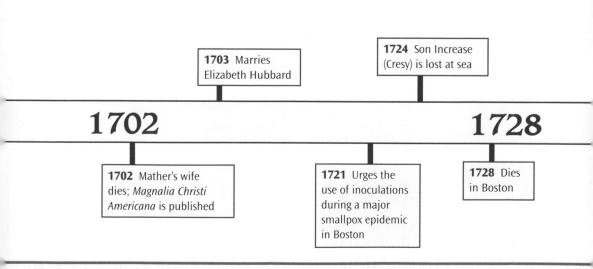

1703 Marries Elizabeth Hubbard

1724 Son Increase (Cresy) is lost at sea

1702

1728

1702 Mather's wife dies; *Magnalia Christi Americana* is published

1721 Urges the use of inoculations during a major smallpox epidemic in Boston

1728 Dies in Boston

"spectral evidence," he strongly supports the trials going forward.

1702   After a lingering illness, Mather's wife dies, probably of tuberculosis. *Magnalia Christi Americana* is published; his most important book, it outlines the history of the New England colonies from Plymouth Rock to the present time in Mather's life.

1703   Marries Elizabeth Hubbard.

1710   Awarded a Doctor of Divinity degree by the University of Glasgow.

1713   Elected as a Fellow of the Royal Society of London.

1721   Urges the use of inoculations during a major smallpox epidemic in Boston. For his efforts, he is unfairly attacked by the general population as well as the medical establishment.

1724   Mather's son Increase (Cresy) is lost at sea.

1726   Mather's daughter Elizabeth dies. She is the thirteenth out of his fifteen children to die.

1728   Cotton Mather dies in Boston. He is buried at the old Copp's Hill Burying Ground.

Bibliography

"Biography of Richard Mather." Classic Encyclopedia. Available online. http://www.1911encyclopedia.org/Richard_Mather.

Demos, John Putnam. *Entertaining Satan: Witchcraft and the Culture of Early New England*. New York: Oxford University Press, 1983.

Gouge, William. *Of Domestical Duties*. Lulu.com, 2006.

Hartley, L.P. *The Go-Between*. New York: NYRB Classics, 2002.

Lutz, Norma Jean. *Cotton Mather: Author, Clergyman, and Scholar*. Philadelphia: Chelsea House Publishers, 2000.

Mather, Cotton. *The Duties of Children to their Parents*. The Spurgeon Archive. Available online: http://www.spurgeon.org/~phil/mather/dut-chi.htm.

Mather, Cotton. *Magnalia Christi Americana*. Google Books. Available online: http://books.google.com/books?id=49JdS7NoSawC&printsec=titlepage&source=gbs_v2_summary_r&cad=0.

Mather, Cotton. *Memorable Providences, Relating to Witchcrafts and Possessions*. Available online. http://www.piney.com/MatherWitch.html.

Mather, Cotton. *The Wonders of the Invisible World: Observations as Well Historical as Theological, upon the Nature, the Number, and the Operations of the Devils*. DigitalCommons@University of Nebraska–Lincoln. Available online. http://digitalcommons.unl.edu/etas/19/.

Middlekauff, Robert. *The Mathers: Three Generations of Puritan Intellectuals, 1596–1728*. New York: Oxford University Press, 1976.

Silva, Alan J. "Increase Mather." The Literary Encyclopedia. Available online. http://www.litencyc.com/php/speople.php?rec=true&UID=2985.

Silverman, Kenneth. *The Life and Times of Cotton Mather*. New York: Welcome Rain Publishers, 2002.

Winthrop, John. "A Model for Christian Charity." Available online. http://religiousfreedom.lib.virginia.edu/sacred/charity.html.

"Witch-Hunts in Puritan New England." Bookrags.com. Available online. http://www.bookrags.com/research/witch-hunts-in-puritan-new-england-wia-01/.

Further Resources

Hawthorne, Nathaniel. *The House of Seven Gables*. New York: Simon and Schuster, 2007.

Jackson, Shirley. *The Witchcraft of Salem Village*. New York: Random House Books for Young Readers, 1987.

Johnson, Claudia Durst. *Daily Life in Colonial New England*. Santa Barbara, Calif.: Greenwood, 2008.

Rinaldi, Ann. *A Break with Charity: A Story About the Salem Witch Trials*. New York: Gulliver Books Paperbacks, 2003.

Vowell, Sarah. *The Wordy Shipmates*. New York: Riverhead Hardcover, 2008.

Picture Credits

PAGE

Index

About the Author

Dennis Abrams is the author of numerous titles for Chelsea House, including biographies of Barbara Park, Nicolas Sarkozy, Xerxes, Rachael Ray, Albert Pujols, Hillary Rodham Clinton, and Georgia O'Keeffe. He attended Antioch College, where he majored in English and communications. A voracious reader since the age of three, Dennis lives in Houston, Texas, with his partner of 21 years, along with their three cats and their dog, Junie B.